016

Physical and mental illness, poverty, unhappiness are often due to immaturity. Here is an easily read book that motivates the reader to . . . . grow up.

I like it. I think you will too.

W. Clement Stone

YOU AND PSYCHIATRY

YOU
AND
PSYCHIATRY

By

WILLIAM C. MENNINGER, M. D.

and

MUNRO LEAF

CHARLES SCRIBNER'S SONS, NEW YORK

INTRODUCTION

This book is, in a way, a war baby. The authors met for the first time in the Army. One was working in the area of public relations and the other in the professional field of psychiatry. They found their jobs overlapped. The public wanted to know about psychiatry and psychiatry needed public understanding. The terrific loss of manpower in the Army and the Navy from psychiatric casualties started them to thinking that there must be some additional approach to helping the people of our nation understand the basic factors of mental health (certainly there have been lots of them).

It was their intention to try to put into simple words and pictures for men in the service some of the daily experiences that were common to many men, which made the going "rugged." Many believed they were alone in feeling the way they did—about discipline, regimentation, privacy, fear, etc. Most of their attitudes were the result of basic personality factors that existed long before their military service. A realization that they were all in the same boat was reassuring. Duty separated the authors before they had a chance to work it out and when they met again it was as civilians.

Today both feel that there is a much wider need for a better understanding of ourselves which could come from some of the knowledge based on technical findings of psychiatry as learned in the last fifty years. They felt it was worth their trying to put into simple words and abbreviated form some of this information which applies to

v

all of us in our daily lives, that are complicated at any time and more so in this period today that we call "Peace."

There are very few adults who have graduated from the public school system of our country who aren't familiar with at least some information on physical hygiene: the necessity of keeping clean, brushing their teeth, getting the right food, fresh air, exercise and rest. They learned it in terms that they could understand. At the same time there are many persons who have no clear understanding of either mental hygiene or their own personalities.

It would take a pretty hard-boiled citizen to say that there isn't any need for this understanding after taking a quick look around him today. Broken homes, juvenile delinquencies, crime waves, group hatreds, riots, political wranglings, suspicion and fear on all sides are not likely to make a thoughtful man or woman very smug about the state of our individual or collective mental health. What goes for the United States, you can double or triple, for too much of the rest of the world.

This book is written in the hope that it will make clear to many the fundamentals of the vital part of living that aren't taken care of by food, tooth paste, soap and water, or any amount of money. Don't have any illusions, however; it is no graduate course in psychiatry. No book can solve your personal problems if they are serious. However, it ought to give you a little better understanding of yourself and how you tick. The chances are it will help you know yourself and other people a little better.

⊷§ FOREWORD §⊷

There are several ways we can look on the stretch of years during which we live on this earth. Some seem to regard it as a knock-down, drag-out fight with no quarter given. Others seem to breeze along having a good time, no matter what happens. Most of us land somewhere in between and take our share of the good times with the bad ones, being happy part of the time and miserable another part.

Whether we look at the individual man's coping with all of the things in the world outside of himself as a battle with that world, an adjustment or an adaptation to it, or as a sort of friendly puppy-like tussle that is good, pleasant exercise, may be as much a matter of philosophy as psychiatry, depending on our point of view.

Any way we play the game of life, the outcome will depend on the strength of the personality. The personality is what other people know as you. It is made up of more than what meets the eye at a quick, or even a long, glance.

Most of us, when we are well and sober, believe that we know why we do what we do. But the psychiatrists tell us that this isn't true, and the evidence seems to stack up all in their favor. If we are quite honest with ourselves, we cannot always see the reasons for our behavior. After a reaction to a particular situation or person we sometimes find ourselves wondering how we could have been so stupid? So rude? So angry? So passive? So silly? We may even be emotionally upset by our concern over the way we behaved. In other words all of us have moments when we know that we don't quite understand ourselves.

How can we learn to behave "normally" and "naturally" and "appropriately"? Those are the questions that the psychiatrist tries to answer for the people who come to see him professionally. All of us need some help every now and then. At least some of the knowledge which the psychiatrist uses can be helpful to anyone who understands it. On the assumption that a lot of people want it, the authors have tried to present such knowledge in easily understandable terms.

This is a presentation of what the psychoanalytic psychiatrists believe the personality is, its development, its structure, its mode of action. In short it is a description of the anatomy and the physiology of the personality. We will try to lift the "average" personality off the street or out of the sitting room and take it to pieces in order to demonstrate its parts and explain how they came to be what they are. We will try to show how that personality operates and some of the results of good or bad operation, as the psychiatrist understands them.

Right at the start we ought to tell you that psychiatry is the branch of medicine, that concerns itself with the study (the diagnosis), the treatment and the prevention of all types of psychological difficulties. The psychiatrist is a physician (an M.D.—"doctor of medicine") who in the course of his medical education and hospital internship did what every other doctor has to do. He learned about bacteria and physiology, set broken bones and did minor surgery, made blood and urine examinations and treated heart cases and diabetes. After all that, he spent five more years in specialized training and experience in the field of psychiatry. Then if he wished to qualify and be listed as a "specialist," he had to take and pass special examinations of the American Board of Neurology and Psychiatry. The statement of these well-known facts is important for the reason that an amazing number of people do not know just what psychiatry is and how a psychiatrist is trained.

In this book are some statements of psychiatric theory and some illustrations of the cause and effect of human behavior. Each reader will probably see himself in the following pages, for the general principles outlined are applicable to us all. For the sake of his orientation certain facts are basic to an accurate understanding of human behavior.

First, it is impossible to describe a "normal" personality for there is no one pattern of development or action that is "ideal" for everyone. *All of us* have eccentricities and neurotic symptoms. Periodically we all have doubts and worries. We have trouble with our children and they have trouble with us. There are hundreds of varieties of personality strengths and handicaps. There are varying degrees and types of adjustment and maladjustment. With our assets and liabilities, or in spite of these, most of us get along reasonably comfortably. Perhaps explanations of the variations and the causes of the handicaps can enable us to live more satisfactorily.

Second, the two energy drives that make us go are aggressiveness and the desire to and need for love. It is the aggressive drive that causes our difficulties. Because of the hostile and destructive element in it, it gets you and me into most of our troubles, whether they concern ourselves or others. Truly loving or being loved (called the erotic drive) never hurts anyone. But all aggression isn't "bad," in fact it takes some aggressiveness to love, as well as most of the other things we do. On the other hand, there are many varieties of relationships in loving and being loved that are not "good." Smothering love, binding love, jealous love—are harmful and become problems because of the type of aggression in them, not because of the love.

Third, the reader should understand that feelings and behavior are chiefly the result of development and train-

ing. Our inheritance does have something to do with the
way in which we develop but by comparison with the
environment it is of minor importance. As we gain more
understanding of ourselves and therefore of our psychological status we can see how we can improve. Unless a
person actually has a defective brain he *can* become more
mature, the ideal goal for every personality. Lots of us
need to grow up psychologically—to forego childish techniques and emotional attachments, to learn to control
ourselves emotionally, to find our greatest satisfaction in
giving rather than in receiving. Therefore, it is the hope
of the authors that as the result of perusing these pages
the reader will increase his knowledge of the personality
and thus perhaps be able to help himself mature and to
deal more intelligently with other people, particularly
the younger generation.

Sufficient understanding of ourselves should make us
more tolerant of the behavior of others. It is so easy to
misjudge or call names and it is so hard to get the mote
out of our own eyes. Would that we had the perspicacity
of a legless combat veteran who made the remark that he
didn't see how he could ever know a buddy well enough
to call him a coward!

A fourth point the authors want to make is that *intellectual acceptance* of the relation between emotional stress
and personality development may aid in solving personal
problems. For example, the misdirection of the aggressive
drive into expressions of hate, stubbornness, meanness,
jealousy and envy—the festering boils in our everyday
lives—can usually be traced to childhood difficulties in
adjustment. The fact that we *know* these emotions are
irrational and have forgotten and obscure origins in infancy *can* provide a basis for some intellectual control.
We don't have to have a complete understanding of their
origin in order to reduce their incidence. While it is
desirable for a fire department to know what started a fire,

it is not necessary to know the cause before trying to put it out. All that *must* be done is to recognize that there is a fire and then do something about it.

There are a thousand homely illustrations of the applications of this principle to human behavior. If running the town or the club interferes with the necessity of running a business or a home we do not have to find the psychological explanation of why we allow ourselves to become too deeply involved. We only have to recognize priorities in our lives and at the same time endeavor to meet the need for inner satisfaction in ways that do not interfere with the "musts."

At the same time we offer reassurance to the readers of their ability to modify childhood-formed patterns of reaction we must warn against expecting too much from their efforts in that direction. Reading a cook book isn't going to change an amateur into a professional chef. Daily brushing of teeth does not prevent all cavities. Perusing this bit of light reading about *some* of our psychological anatomy and how it functions isn't going to make us into 100% well-adjusted personalities automatically.

As much as we all wish for it, there isn't anyone (including the authors of this book!) who is qualified to hand out neat little prescriptions that are guaranteed to cure all aches, pains, worries and fears. Here and there the reader will find some specific leads to a better understanding which may—we say *may*—enable him to live more easily with the day-by-day reactions of his family, his friends and himself.

Smooth sailing in life depends not on placebos and panaceas but on the craft (our personalities), the weather (the temper of our associates), and the navigation (our skill in steering a wise course).

ᏜᎦ CONTENTS Ꮬ

YOU AND PSYCHIATRY

CHAPTER I

OUR MACHINERY

MOST PEOPLE know something about the human body—that it has a digestive system, a heart, a pair of lungs, and a lot of other systems and organs that are very important. Some of these we all talk about more or less intelligently. Others we discuss only hesitantly. However, at the mere mention of one, many people get cross.

The organ located in our heads, known as the brain, is well known. But even about it people get mixed up and talk about "having lots of brains" as if there were several of them or perhaps thinking of it as they would wheat or potatoes. Actually, a man has *a* brain which weighs a little over two pounds. In proportion to the size of the body, it is larger in man than in any other animal. We know it has much to do with thinking and feeling and acting, but actually we cannot locate many functions in specific areas or parts of it.

It is divided into two "hemispheres." In general, the right one controls the left half of the body and the left controls the right half of the body. In each hemisphere there is a little area about the size of a pocket knife that controls all of our motor activity and one of similar small size that registers sensation. The area that controls speech isn't much bigger than a dime and is located on the oppo-

1

site side from our "handedness": if you are right-handed,
it is on the left side of your brain; if left-handed it is on
the right side. In the back part is another small area that
has to do with vision. At least two-thirds of the surface
of the brain, however, is "terra-incognito" insofar as any
specific function is concerned.

To and from the brain go a lot of nerves, like telegraph
wires. Some of them run to the eyes, the ears and the
tongue and other parts of the head. There are twelve of
these—the cranial nerves. Then the great bulk of telegraph
wires combine into one solid trunk that we call the spinal
cord which runs down inside our backbone. At the level
of each vertebra, a pair of nerves flow out to cover the
adjacent area of the body.

Very simply there are three sets of nerves that connect
up the brain, through the spinal cord, with the muscles,
the skin and all the organs inside of us. One of these sets
takes the incoming calls such as the sensations of touch
or pain or temperature which are received by any part
of the body; another group takes over the message from
these incoming wires and conducts them up to the headquarters—the brain. The third set is the outgoing bunch
that produces action. They are the ones that start us doing
something about a particular situation.

The networks of nerves serve two nervous systems. One
of these is the *autonomic* or the *involuntary nervous system*. This system controls and regulates the action of most
of our organs, including the heart, stomach, intestines,
blood vessels and sweat glands. It has both direct and
indirect connections with the *voluntary nervous system*
(brain, spinal cord and nerves) which helps us do what
we *think* we want to do, whether it is moving an arm,
taking a walk or making a speech. To illustrate the fact
that there is no voluntary control of the autonomic nervous system, put a spoonful of food in your mouth and
see how much control you have over what happens to it

from there on. Or, try to prevent yourself from blushing or stop it once started.

These nerve connections are very complicated. There are a lot of short-cuts possible so that sometimes a message comes into the spinal cord that never has to go up to general headquarters—the brain—but connects up directly with the outgoing nerves that produce action. Thus, if you tap yourself just below the kneecap, with your leg crossed, the chances are that your foot will kick. In this case the sensation goes into the spinal cord and then right at the same level connects up with the nerves that go to the muscle and produce action. This sort of response is called *reflex* and the machinery which produces it is known as a *reflex arc*.

There are a lot of different types of reflexes. They are very important to the physician in his examination because they are sensitive to slight changes. Some of the ones present in the healthy individual disappear in sickness, and others develop as a result of nerve disease. In all cases they represent a direct connection between the sensory and motor nerves so that the impulse never has to go through the "higher centers" to produce action.

Another type of somewhat automatic behavior comes as the result of experience. Much of it seems to become reflex although we originally had to learn what to do. For example, the initial discovery that fire was hot and that it hurt connected up the nerve pathways so strongly that later messages about fire could get fast action. Pulling a finger off a hot stove isn't a reflex but it is illustrative of behavior that becomes automatic and takes place without thinking, *a conditioned reflex*.

So far, all we have said has to do with machinery that you can examine in anatomical specimens and under the microscope. The fact remains, however, that there is a big gap between this physical machinery and the thinking, feeling, acting person. Scientists are still a long way from being able to explain the thinking and feeling of people entirely on the basis of our knowledge about the brain or nerve anatomy and physiology.

Unquestionably, much of this activity goes on in the brain but the brain is only a part of the total mechanism. The endocrine glands, such as the thyroid, adrenals, ovaries, testicles and others whose secretions pass directly into the blood affect one's behavior. The process of metabolism is another factor. It is the process by which we build up and break down our body tissues, some of us slowly and some of us rapidly. A major influence on the development of our physical structure, including brain and spinal cord (and therefore our thinking-feeling-acting self), is what we get from our parents—our inheritance.

Thinking is not just a matter of brain cell activity, emotion isn't just glandular activity, and action isn't just muscle activity. They are all inescapably bound together. Consequently one cannot spell out, even in a complicated explanation, a complete description of the total machinery of the person in order to explain how he thinks and feels and acts.

Even though the psychiatrist does not know enough about the anatomy of the personality to explain all these reactions, he can and does make observations about the psychological life which can be arranged in a systematic fashion. Such a study is not a description of the machinery but rather a classification of various expressions of the total person. In addition to the physical and chemical aspects, the psychiatrist systematically investigates the psychological aspects of the personality. Most of these are only the conscious expressions of the personality in response to its internal and external demands. There are several different systems of organization of such data. One convenient classification of psychological life has four divisions—Perception, Intellection, Emotion and Volition.

PERCEPTION: Perception is the psychological activity

involved in the receiving and the interpretation of sensations from the sense organs—eyes, ears, nose, mouth and skin. Once received, these sensations automatically are referred up to the General Headquarters in the brain. There, on the basis of past experience, they are recognized and interpreted. The interpretation may be an automatic recognition if it's an old sensation. If it's a new one, it is compared with old ones.

There are lots of variations in the acuteness and accuracy of perception in ordinary life. Much of this variation depends upon an individual's past experience; it depends on the degree of alertness; sometimes it depends on the nature of physical phenomena. Everyone has periods when he's a little confused or disoriented, as for instance when awakened suddenly from a deep sleep. On the other hand, everyone has moments or situations in which he is hyper-alert and can hear or see more acutely. Then there are those natural phenomena such as mirages and other types of what are known as optical illusions which prevent our sensations from telling us the truth. There are variations in the capacities of persons to perceive, some of which are inherited and others of which are dependent on the physical machinery. For instance some people are born blind to color; that's usually an inherited trait. Some of us can see much better at night than others. Some people have a special ability to hear musical tones of a very high pitch. Many special capacities can be specially cultivated so that the blind man's fingers can become sufficiently sensitive to make up in some degree for his lack of sight; the wine taster's taste buds become sensitive to differences that most of us would ordinarily miss; some people can stand pain more stoically than others.

The second large field of psychological life is called INTELLECTION. That includes the thinking processes, as well as the storehouse of memories, called knowledge.

Intellection also includes intelligence—one's ability to use the knowledge that he has accumulated. A lack of intelligence is stupidity; a lack of knowledge is ignorance. Intellection is therefore our knowledge, our ideas, our reasoning ability, our day dreams, as well as the dreams we have at night.

There are many individual variations in intellection which cannot be understood merely in terms of the function of the physical machinery. There isn't any anatomical explanation as to why one member of a family makes good use of intelligence and another has a much lesser capacity in this field. One can test the memory span, i.e. how long one can remember an eight-digit figure, but we do not know why it differs in two people otherwise very similar. Some of us are inclined to hold onto old ideas; others have a continuous stream of new ones. Sometimes a certain idea gets "fixed" and we can't forget it; the same idea keeps recurring to us or perhaps a tune keeps running through our minds. Some of us live too much in our day dreams and others claim they have none. Some of us seem to be active all night in our dreams and other people will swear that they never dream. Some of us become delirious with a low fever; others remain clear with a high one.

Making decisions is one of our intellectual activities. All of us have to make them every day, really hundreds of times. Sometimes they are unimportant and sometimes they are terribly important. Sometimes we avoid or delay doing so, more or less successfully. We want but we don't want; we should but somehow we can't; we will but we should not. This state of affairs psychiatrists label as *conflict*. In most instances the forces in favor of one side are so strong that we act, right or wrong. The really tough decisions get all tied up with a third area of our conscious psychological life—our *emotions*.

EMOTION. In simplest terms, our emotions are our

feelings. A lot of times they overrule our intelligence. They vary greatly in their expression, but all of them are sub-species of hate or love or fear. Much of our thinking and behavior becomes involved in our emotions. If it didn't, life would be pretty drab.

As we will learn later on, at certain stages we pick out certain persons in whom we invest love or hate. Some of us have a lot of emotion to invest; some of us are acutely deficient in it. Even those of us who have a lot of it are aware sometimes that we run out of it—we lose interest, we grow apathetic, we get "browned off." This apparent deficiency sometimes represents a transition from a positive to a negative reaction, a shift from love to hate.

Not only are the emotions bound up with our thinking but they are inseparably linked to the rest of the body. The emotions perhaps more than any other psychological activity involve the function of the entire body. Through the nervous machinery, the whole physical structure is notified and very often specific parts of it will promptly react as a part of the total emotional response. For instance, an emotion like fear stimulates, through the nervous system machinery, the adrenal glands that sit right on top of the kidneys. These respond by turning loose a secretion, adrenalin, that raises the blood pressure, makes the heart beat faster and tenses the muscles. There are many different types of physical responses to emotion: Embarrassment may result in blushing; anger may stop the secretion of digestive juices; tenseness may make the palms of our hands sweat.

Emotional responses are awfully complicated, not only as to variety, the object toward which they are directed, and the way they are manifest, but also by the fact that they can't be measured and very often they are difficult or impossible to control. This is in part due to the structure of the personality, which we will discuss later. For instance, we all know people who cry when they're happy.

Most of us get mad when we ought to stay calm. Some of us get blue over unimportant matters or even for no apparent reason. Often we can't control our trembling or our shakiness even after the episode which stimulated it is over.

VOLITION. A large area of psychological life has to do with willful behavior. We have seen that many of our internal organs are entirely involuntary in their action. On the other hand, most of our body muscles are largely under voluntary control. So, we speak or move our arms or walk or jump up and down or sit still if, when, and because we want to do so.

A great deal of what we do becomes set in grooves or patterns that we call *habits.* The way we add up a column of figures, how we organize the day's schedule, how we greet people—all follow a plan which has been established by frequent use. Behavior that is a part of our daily lives becomes semi-automatic—how we shave, how we sit down on a chair, how we wash the dishes. Our mannerisms and our method of speech are habits. Some habits are regarded as good or bad depending on our point of view—eating sweets, chewing gum, smoking, getting up late in the morning after breakfast in bed, saving money.

Habits are, of course, economical in energy use because they save us effort in thinking about what to do or how. We get "set" in our ways. That is efficient except when the habit itself isn't any good or is even harmful. Then it is sometimes difficult to dislodge it and institute a new or better way.

The natural end product of much of our conscious life is our *behavior.* At the same time we have to recognize that a lot of our action isn't entirely rational. We do many things without being able to understand why we do them. In fact, often we are puzzled by our own actions. Yet, *we* performed them. Our apparently voluntary behavior actually isn't regulated very much by conscious thought. In fact our perception, intellection, emotion and action are all greatly influenced by our unconscious. More of that later.

Behavior is really the product of the combined processes of perception, intellection and emotion. For example, we perceive a man coming towards us with a gun. Our eyes see him and size him up as a rowdy character; our knowledge and experience tell us that we are in danger; this intellectual activity then gets linked up immediately with the appropriate emotion—fear (or courage) —and this then is conveyed to the glands and muscles of our body. We call on our judgment to evaluate the situation, and finally we act. A more common illustration is what happens to us when we come into the house in the evening and smell a beef steak cooking. The sensation is perceived, intellectually compared and identified with past experience, and the emotion associated with the psychological need—hunger—starts the gastric juice flowing in our stomach. It isn't hard to guess the behavior it will produce.

For many years psychiatrists have been treating people whose psychological machinery has broken down. From careful study of what happens in illness and what is found to have contributed toward its initial onset, they have learned a very great deal about why we do what we do. They are beginning to be able to formulate some general principles for the guidance of those who are in good health mentally. Certain practices which assist the ill person to return to health are equally applicable to the well person who wants to stay well. These are the basis of the following pages.

~§ CHAPTER II §~

OUR ORIENTATION

ANYTHING WE do, any move we make in life, more often than not, is started by impulses inside us that come from somewhere other than that relatively small portion of us we call our conscious mind. Arthur Merriweather who starts downtown to buy his Francine some flowers to wear on their date, but instead winds up shooting pool with the boys, will have a tough time explaining to her why he didn't get to the florist. But he will have a still rougher time trying to spell it all out to himself. He knows perfectly well that when he went downtown he *really* meant to get those flowers. He loves his Francie and he will be glad to argue with you if you say he doesn't.

The next time you dial the phone to tell the butcher you want some meat, and the voice that answers on the other end is that of the hair dresser, you might as well go ahead and spend your husband's hard-earned money for that permanent you want so badly. But just don't tell anyone that *you never* do anything you don't *know* about.

Some of us are curious about W H Y we decide suddenly, one day in the shower, to take out more insurance. W H Y do we want to go to the mountains this summer instead of down to the beach where we've listened to the

waves every year since Agnes had scarlet fever. Those
Why's and all the Why's of human behavior have beginnings that rarely, if ever, are up there on the surface. The
overwhelming majority of our decisions and actions are
the external result of our mental activity. They are like
the foam on the beer.

To begin to understand why we do what we do, we
must go back to what happened to each one of us a long
time ago. But before we start trying to put into words the
meaning of our early experience, let's talk about the
words themselves that we will have to use.

If you or I tried to sit in on a discussion group of
electronic engineers hashing over some improvements in
radar and they started jabbering in that dialect they call
technical language, it wouldn't take us very long to find
out that the shop words they used were confusing us
even if we were capable of following the main line of
their ideas.

Well, the same applies to the language of people who
work in this field of psychiatry. An extreme example
would be the argument as to whether that patient in
Ward C manifests a catatonic type of schizophrenia or a
manic phase of a manic-depressive psychotic reaction. The
verbiage they use makes it tough sometimes for the average layman to stay with them.

Unfortunately psychiatric terms sometimes become a
handicap for the better understanding of psychiatry. Lay-
men pick them up from popular articles—articles that use
the terms but do not adequately or correctly explain them.
Then the person thinks he knows the term and what it
means, uses it incorrectly, and more people are confused.

The confusion and haze that hang over practically any
word that has *psych* in it is interesting but often downright discouraging. Derived from the Greek word Psyche.
the term somehow came to mean the *soul* and later the
mind.

The fears and shames surrounding the popular conceptions and misconceptions of mental illness have, for many people, tainted all the *psych*-terms. As a result most people are much more comfortable with the vague but to them nicer sounding expressions like nervous breakdown, and in war, shell shock or combat exhaustion than any label that has *psych* attached to it.

Thousands who will cheerfully bore you by the hour with blow-by-blow accounts of their most intimate surgical operations often shy like a colt at any mention of their seeking professional help in the adjustment of their personality to their environment. But there is a little light in the darkness. The benefits from psychiatry are becoming better known. The war experience educated millions of military personnel and their families. There is a rapidly increasing number of people who are seeking psychiatric advice about their everyday problems, a long time before they might "blow their tops."

Nevertheless, in some ways, the attitude towards the study of people's ideas and behavior at the present time is just about where the study of the body was a few centuries ago when it was sinful and against the law to dissect the human body. Despite the then current taboos of law and religion some of the earliest anatomists hid themselves out and worked at night in order to add to medical science for the benefit of mankind. The whole study of the human race in relation to the mind and behavior has been and is still handicapped miserably by taboos, bugaboos, stupidity, prudery, deceit and out-and-out pigheadedness.

There are reasons for these misconceptions and taboos about mental ill health. Psychiatry as a science is young. Even in comparison with other branches of medicine it's one of the babies. Only a little more than 150 years ago people with mental illness were accused of being witches or thought to be possessed by animals. They were thrown into unsanitary, unlighted, unkept prisons. They were exhibited for a fee, like animals at the circus, in order to get a pittance with which to feed them.

For hundreds of years disorders of behavior were in varying ways tied up with religion. By some people, mental sickness was regarded as a punishment for sin. Others considered it as a sin itself.

However, it wasn't just because of religion, that many people did and too many still do regard many types of unusual behavior as perversity, cussedness, meanness or insanity. This lack of knowledge about the cause of strange actions and the apparent inability to correct or improve them made it easier to shut people so afflicted out of sight, and therefore out of mind than to protect and care for them.

The doctors who tried to ameliorate their fate were also isolated, were not given means to treat or even to house and feed their patients decently, to say nothing of providing for research about them. In fact, this state of affairs continues today.

Various leaders in medicine began making spectacular discoveries like the circulation of the blood, the bacterial cause of disease, the contagiousness of certain diseases, the use of the microscope. Medicine developed a strong trend toward becoming chiefly a physical science. Many doctors still find it far more satisfying to study an electrical tracing of the heartbeat than to attempt to understand the effect on the heart beat of those intangible things called the emotions. For still there are not very many quantitative measuring rods or scales that have proven useful in evaluating human behavior.

Finally, there isn't any doubt that the refusal to understand or investigate mental ill health is directly associated with our own emotions. One of the very real obstacles to the acceptance of psychiatry is the inherent fear in all of us that we might need it ourselves. We are afraid that study might reveal us to be "not quite right" or maybe even a little "queer." We are too familiar with the shushed tone of voice and superior attitude of the gossip who, at the bridge club, starts the whisper about how her friend went to see the psychiatrist, with the insinuation that such an act is proof of the friend's craziness. Such persons never have any recognition of their own need nor that their inference clearly indicates their fears about themselves.

Psychiatry received its greatest boost towards becoming a scientific method from one man, Sigmund Freud, just a little over fifty years ago. Doctor Freud was a neurologist, a specialist in diseases of the organic nervous system. He became interested in why people behave the way they do. Along with a fellow-Viennese physician, Brewer, he began investigating. Although Brewer first used the "cathartic method," Freud was responsible for the creation of "psychoanalysis." This has turned out to be one of the most helpful research approaches, one of the best treatment methods and certainly the best theory of the explanation of human behavior. But again, as the result of Freud's efforts, psychiatry bumped head on into more resistance to its acceptance. Most intelligent people know something of Freud. They have at least heard his name. But there are an amazing number of persons who firmly believe that he was some filthy-minded old man who said, "People don't think about anything but sex, SEX, S E X."

In 1917 Freud forecast that there would be a lot of opposition to some of the special features of psychoanalysis. He knew that they would arouse anxiety and prejudice because they would necessarily wound human self-esteem in some degree. Specifically, the admission and acceptance of the power of the unconscious means that "the Ego is not master in its own house." No one likes to face the fact that he does not know himself or that he has no real understanding of much of his behavior. Freud pointed out that twice before mankind had resisted humiliations arising from the development of scientific knowledge—when Copernicus proved that the earth is not the center of the universe, and when Darwin demonstrated that man is an animal.

Among many other things, Freud certainly did talk about sex. He regarded it as a natural human phenomenon which motivates a tremendous part of life. However, he was much more inclusive in his meaning of the word sex and didn't limit it, as most Americans do, to genital activities. Probably of as great importance as his contributions to understanding sexual development, if not more so, were Freud's many contributions toward our understanding of the unconscious, the mental anatomy and machinery by which we function, the origin and actions of our conscience, the importance of certain events in infantile and childhood development and many other points.

Many are the misconceptions about psychiatry. Some are due entirely to ignorance. Some are based on resentment against something that the resenter has never bothered to try to understand. Some are based on opposition to the fact that our actions aren't always under our complete conscious control. The result of all of these has been a wide-spread hodge-podge of stupidity and belligerence towards increased understanding or scientific study of man and his *psyche* or *mind*. Now the tide seems to be turning and with hungry eagerness, the public cries for more and more knowledge about and assistance in the maintenance of mental health.

CHAPTER III

OUR TRAINING

OUR FIRST ten years are the big ones. Fortunately for most of us, our parents stay around to help us get started in this contest called life, and those of us who have kind, loving, intelligent mothers and fathers are the truly blessed.

If they handle us well in childhood, most of us can take the rest of the journey right along in our stride. That's because the biggest factor in the mental health of an adult is the pattern that was set during the first years of life.

By six or seven years of age the personality is pretty well jelled. If, at your present age, you're honest or dishonest, reliable or unreliable, accept authority or defy it, get along with people or not—try to remember back to you when you were in about the fourth or fifth grade and you'll find the two *yous* have a lot in common. If you have trouble now with the things and the people around you, it's a safe bet the roots of that trouble were planted back there in those first ten years of life.

When a baby first sees the light of day, he does not care about any one beyond himself. He is out to find the answer to, "What's in it for me?" He has certain instincts at birth and all he wants in life is to satisfy them. In the

16

early months he doesn't give anything to anybody nor try to please any one. In short, he doesn't care about anything but getting what he wants when he wants it.

He is not going to accommodate his mother by waiting until seven a.m. for his feeding. He doesn't take into consideration that momentarily he is being held in the arms of a fond visitor with a pretty silk dress on. He speaks up in one way or another even if mother *is* busy or guests are present. He pretty well succeeds in making the world revolve about him.

He works on a very neat and simple basis of putting all his efforts into one double-barreled urge:

"Get all the *Pleasure* I can."
"Get out of all the *Pain* I can."

And by *Pain* he doesn't mean just a safety pin sticking him or some other physical suffering, but every other sort of displeasure, unhappiness and discomfort as well.

For the better part of the first year, the baby's chief interest and form of gratification is in receiving his milk. Nothing else amounts to a hill of beans from where he sits, or lies, rather. His whole life is bound up in this one source of satisfaction.

Toward the end of his first year, he gets a new interest. Usually his parents (most often his mother) start to try to control his output of that food and drink as well as its intake. In this job of toilet-training baby, his attention is focused on these processes and they become his chief bodily interest. This new learning diverts his interest in some degree from the previously all-absorbing interest he had in using his mouth.

Through the baby's second year and usually the third, too, nobody has a right to be surprised and/or shocked if he is interested in his process of evacuation (going to the toilet to get rid of the waste matter that comes out of his anus).

The next shift of his main interest is the one that be-comes a source of great concern to a lot of parents. Some parents are stupid; some ignorant; but a lot of intelligent and sincere ones get powerfully upset. Just as surely as the sun will set tonight and come up again tomorrow morning, the boy baby will realize that he has sexual organs and the girl baby will find that she has a certain section of her body that holds a very special interest for her.

At about the age of three years this will come as a discovery filled with natural, powerful interest. If they have curiosity about their own sexual anatomy and those of others around them—what they're for—how and why are they different—you don't need to worry about them; if they *don't* have curiosity, then you have cause to worry.

So it goes, and so it went with everyone of us. Every infant goes through three major stages of development, all of which occur in his first three, or at most four, years. Each of them concerns a specific part of his anatomy which is temporarily of primary interest to the baby. Three areas—the mouth, the sphincters, and the genital apparatus not only become the objects of very special attention but experiences associated with them become the origin of techniques in gaining satisfaction and han-dling frustrations.

The young human being focuses primarily on the "oral zone" for about the first year; then the "anal zone," roughly for the second and third years; and finally on the "genital zone" from the third year, as a rule, to about the sixth.

These three stages have far more significance than merely the physical gratifications or satisfactions or, on the other hand, the frustrations that the child experiences. The activities involved, namely the way the child learns to eat, the toilet training, the parental management of the sexual curiosity and activity, are the basis of all later relationships to other people. They establish the patterns of the way he will engage their interests, support and hostility, patterns that he will follow as long as he lives. It is through the relation with his parents during these events that he learns (or fails to learn) what it is to be loved; he begins to love; he develops the techniques that bind and hold him to people and people to him.

Nobody can make any hard and fast rules on just when the child is going to shift from one of these experiences to the other. This depends greatly on his parental management. There are certainly no iron curtains between the "stages" and the techniques of one period are often carried over to another.

Freud called these the *psychosexual stages of development* and that is the term they still go by. This term means that along the way of psychological development the infant passes milestones as the urges and forces inside of this new person try to relate him to the people about him and find techniques that give him satisfaction.

In a book like this, we can't do much more than hit the high spots of these three vitally important experiences in our development. There is nothing to stop you from reading and studying more about them and their influences in one's life in many technically written books. These stages are very important in determining our personality and character traits because throughout our lives we go on using the techniques learned then—at least those that seem to work.

ORAL STAGE

For about the first year, unless the parents introduce the second experience of toilet training into this year, the baby's feeding process has the top priority for interest This makes the baby's mouth the important contact with the world. Not only does he use it to pull in food to ease that tension in his insides, but he also takes in his mother's affection at the same time. The main event every three or four hours is meal time, and the one who cuddles him while feeding him by breast or bottle, in the long run, is just as important as the food. The little baby is certain to have a warm feeling for that person as long as she takes good care of him.

Absorbing the food is pleasant, but if we look more closely there is still a lot more to it than that. The sucking it in is fun too. The researchers who track down these things have shown that the bottle-fed baby who tosses off his meal in comparatively quick time is more likely to be a thumbsucker later than is the one who gets his milk more frequently, more naturally and more slowly from the breast. Along this same point, it is probable that the extra amount of cuddling and loving is very important too.

Sometimes we can distinguish between two phases in the oral stage of development, the early sucking phase and later the biting phase. Any mother who tried to nurse her child and had difficulty supplying enough milk to satisfy his growing needs can tell you all about this. The biting stage occurs after the baby has developed some pretty firm gums and even beginning little teeth. It is presumed to be an indication of impatience or frustration, of which mother is made painfully aware.

There isn't sufficient scientific data to prove clearly the relation of these "oral" experiences to adult behavior. On the other hand, there is some presumptive evidence that mother-child relationship may lead to passivity in some of us and aggressivity in others. Certainly there is no doubt that there are individuals who are dependent hangers-on, who never quit "sucking" to get everything they can from everybody. There are also personalities who seem to keep on biting all the rest of their lives. As small children their best weapon seems to be their teeth. As adults they stay argumentative, acid, and sarcastic. Most of us seem to come in between the "suckers" and the "biters" with milder tendencies in both directions.

As adults a good many of the techniques we use to find satisfaction through this physical machinery undoubtedly have their relationship to early life experience. Smoking is a definite carry-over from this mouth-centered stage. As we watch some of our pals suck cigarette holders and chew on their cigars and pipes, pens, pencils, eyeglasses, etc. we only need to open our minds to see the connection with their baby days. Gum chewing is one of the commonest practices of the adult who is still searching for oral gratification. Probably some of the saddest humans are the infant-like and childishly irresponsible men and women who cling to the substitute for the original bottle when it contains alcohol instead of milk.

Much more important though than the physical methods of gratification are those aspects of this experience which relate us to people. There isn't any doubt that it is from this life experience that we build up the traits of either optimism or pessimism. It isn't by accident that Santa Claus is always fat and that dyspepsia and pessimism are so often associated. The oral phase has a lot to do with the degree of our dependence or our independence in adulthood. We know that it relates and equates food and love through the rest of our lives. It was our introduction to the technique of receiving or getting or taking. In our later experiences we use the same methods of getting along with people as we learned in those early lessons.

Another way of explaining the importance of this period in our lives as a method of relating ourselves to those around us is to point out the absence of demands being made of us. Initially, there were simply none. We received love which was totally unsolicited—that is, if we had an even break on the kind of parents we had. Without exertion on our part, we received everything for nothing in return—cuddling, food, attention. We didn't have to work or "earn" any of it. Everything was gratuitous. We played a completely passive role on the receiving end. We all have a streak—in some of us much broader than in others— of using that same technique all through life. A surprising number of adults somehow assume the world owes them a living. Our infantile experience in receiving contributed heavily to the amount of passivity and dependency that each of us show as adults.

Of one thing psychiatrists are very sure: abundant love and protection as expressed in physical proximity and fondling are of prime importance. This is in direct opposition to the school of behaviorist psychology which led mothers to believe it wrong to hold or caress their babies too much. Our belief now is that this can't happen. A mother can't give the baby too much affection.

The best advice, at present, is that newborn infants should be kept in the same room with their mothers in the hospital instead of being separated in a nursery for the first two weeks of their lives. Mothers *should* breast-feed their children whenever this is physically possible. The emotional needs of the baby are as important as his physical needs. For this reason a bottle is a very poor substitute for the breast. If the mother has to resort to a bottle she should certainly hold her baby while he is nursing.

Our best leads now indicate very clearly that an infant doesn't have to be regimented to a schedule. He will develop his own meal-time rhythm within a comparatively short time. Too many mothers assume that they must follow a rigid feeding schedule which ignores the infant's individual needs. Because our practical life as adults requires us to eat at certain hours is no reason why we should expect our babies to do this the moment they are born. No other species in the animal family does it.

One might gain the impression in these suggestions regarding the feeding program that the parents have to lead a very slavish life, with the baby taking over, in order to have everything *his* way. Such is not intended nor is such indicated. There is no gainsaying the fact that bringing a baby through his first three or four years is nigh onto a full-time job for any mother (even though some find ways of doing otherwise). But there is no reason why she and the family should be totally discommoded by the baby. They are bound to be somewhat so— but gradually and as soon as he is able to do so baby has to learn to give; he, too, has to learn to accommodate. The main point about the suggestions is that regimentation is to be avoided; his rhythms can soon be adapted to family living. Just don't try to establish them too rigidly and too early.

ANAL STAGE

The next set of experiences of major importance in the shaping of our characters and our relationships with people is toilet training. As during the previous phase attention is focused not only on a specific part of the anatomy but upon an important function related to it. Attitudes developed vary widely, depending on what the parents think is the best practice and the system of training they use.

In our culture discussion of the process of evacuation is taboo. Although it may enter our personal musings, it is excluded as a subject of interpersonal communication or consideration. In some earlier cultures the equally personal process of eating was circumscribed by social ruling.

Certainly any child can sense that toilet training is very important to his mother and father (or why should they make such a fuss about it?). He early learns that whether he does or doesn't perform has a lot to do with whether he gets approval, love, and is "mama's big boy" or is plain "naughty." If he happens to feel vindictive or willful and stubborn, it is just too bad for everyone. Nevertheless, he is the one who makes the decision, and as any mother will tell you, he *knows* it mighty early in the game. This is one procedure that *he* controls.

Because in this matter baby can do as he wishes in spite of parents who wish him to do their bidding, this training is even more important in some ways than the oral phase in its determination of relationships with the parents. Many parents have time and again had the experience of having begged, pleaded, coaxed, threatened, and even demanded, but all to no avail. Then as soon as baby was removed from the toilet, he performed. Already baby had learned to express his disapproval or hate; he had already learned his first lesson in being stubborn, in having his own way.

On the other hand, those same parents have watched him perform to the encouragement of "be a big boy" or some such cajoling. Baby soon learns that by doing what mother wishes he gets love and approval.

Taboos, prejudices and customs have made many of us turn our backs on other features in this stage of our development. If we observe a tiny human being honestly, we can see that he is not only interested in the process of discharge and what it does in his life but he is also interested in the product. He created that stuff, liquid or solid, and what's more, all the shushing, slapping and scolding in the world isn't going to kill his interest in that creation.

There isn't any doubt that the experiences connected with toilet training and the resultant relationships towards the parents establish the forerunners of many attitudes and practices in our later life. We still cannot "prove" that there is a direct link between the specific events that occurred in a particular individual's life in childhood and many of the techniques, attitudes and character traits of his adult life. It is not our purpose to marshal here such of the scientific data as has emerged in the course of psychiatric treatment and shows convincing evidence of some connections. But we will pass on to you the currently accepted opinions of the experts.

They say that this experience was the first by which we learned to *earn* love, praise and approval. It should not stretch anyone's credulity to see it as an adjustment to social demands. The important part of that adjustment really was made to the people who were making those social demands—our parents. Their techniques in teaching us and our response to those techniques undoubtedly cut deep grooves in our developing personalities. Later behavior patterns and relationships followed in those paths.

Many details in the experience influenced our subsequent behavior. Its special importance for most of us was that it was our introduction to regularity and cleanliness. At least it was the first procedure that impressed these characteristics upon our consciousness. From this process some of us learned to "stick with a job until it is done," undoubtedly related to perseverance and persistence in later life.

It also fed our sense of power. The actual expression of that power, however, was often a kind of defiance, and with it went the initial expression of stubbornness. Along with bawling when we didn't get our milk or spitting out the orange juice we didn't like, this was one of our earliest opportunities to assert our aggressiveness. Initially, this expression of aggressiveness may only have frustrated mother but it taught us another effective way to use our power. Lots of people as adults gain real satisfaction from frustrating others or even from hurting them. Probably no one would be willing to swear that he had never done so himself. We all know of a few people who seem to work at this process day in and day out.

As we indicated the infant soon learns that his product is important; that it has a very special value for him. He learns that hoarding it sometimes not only annoys his mother but gives him some satisfaction in doing so. Through long detailed evolutionary steps there is evidence to suggest that this first type of hoarding has something to do with the later satisfaction in collecting. This connection is a little easier to see when collecting itself becomes hoarding. It is well illustrated by the miserly old hermit who hoards and piles up his money while he makes the county feed his own mother; the chances are it is the way he learned to frustrate her when he was a baby.

When pointed out to us it isn't difficult to see the relation between the infant's over-evaluation of his product and the various ways we over-evaluate some of our creations in adult life, whether they are our children or the footstool we made. It is a bit jarring to point out that our American vernacular is rich in intuitive recognition of hangovers from infantile life, in this case showing the equation of money or value to this anal phase of development. Most people know what one means when he talks about the "throne" or the "throne room." They can understand the deeper significance of such phrases as "stinking rich," "the pot of gold" or "filthy lucre."

You can easily find people who will snort at many of these suggested tie-ups between our infantile experience and our adult life. They can raise all of the resistance they want or decry the lack of "proof." The fact is, we don't find the snorters among the professional men and women whose life work has given them the opportunity to study human behavior—in health as well as when the machinery is broken, worn down, or has missed a beat under the strain of too heavy a load.

You ask, "Well what can we do about it?" There again, scientific study is not far enough along to enable us to make statements about how to correct or avoid some of the unhealthy adult expressions of a baby's experience in relating himself to mother and father. Perhaps as wise a rule as any would be: Be as natural about the whole procedure as you can. In the first place, it is ill-advised nonsense which certainly stores up trouble for us to try to force the young baby to perform at the parent's demand. Placing baby on the pot and insisting on his sitting there until he evacuates is bound to instil undesirable character traits. Undoubtedly a child *can be* prevented from soiling his panties during his first year but only if the parent takes advantage of natural rhythm. Current scientific information is that at that age he is emotionally and physiologically too young to assume responsibility for sphincter control.

No primitive culture makes anywhere near the fuss about early control that we do. When ready, the baby will, with sympathetic guidance, assume that responsibility in short order. In the meantime he should be given a chance to become familiar with the toilet without too much emphasis on its use. Bowel training can probably best start some time about the end of the first year or during the second year.

A word about the adult attitude towards the regularity of evacuation. Partly because of our early training and instruction in physical hygiene, partly perhaps because of a long-established daily rhythm in ourselves, and partly because of an unconscious over-evaluation of the process, many, many adults assume that daily bowel evacuation is essential to health. Therefore, when this doesn't occur in their babies they are concerned. It is surprising news to many persons that the normal evacuation rhythm in many adults is every second, third, fourth or even fifth day. No damage is done when it doesn't occur routinely every day. The unfortunate result for the children of those parents who feel that it must occur daily, is the free use of suppositories and enemas. Psychologically speaking, unless the child is ill or there is some evidence of his being unhealthy, enemas are something to be avoided. Even grumpiness or lassitude should not be an automatic signal for a mother to reach for the suppository. Most babies, children and adults will establish a rhythm of their own. In spite of the psychological need of the parents, they should avoid making a fetish out of daily regularity by setting a precise hour and minute that the procedure should occur.

Bladder training can start early in the second year. It takes a little longer than bowel training; at least there are more apt to be "accidents," particularly at times of emotional stress after baby has some semblance of control.

Sphincter control, including its release, is a learned ability. A parental aid is to commend success in its achievement. Punishment is never in order, nor is shaming. With an older child discussion of the problem sometimes accompanied by sympathetic approval of effort helps. In general, when the child is old enough, physically and emotionally, he will "train" quickly. In the meantime, any "dryness" of which a mother brags is the result of her ability to get the child and toilet together at the proper interval.

GENITAL STAGE

In every human being at about the age of three or four years there wells up a sexual curiosity, and with it a certain amount of sexual excitement. Prudes, who seem to refuse to believe that people are human beings, often get upset about this.

When a child expresses this natural curiosity, asks questions and tries to investigate a little he, too, often gets squelched and even punished. What should be the finest

and noblest joys of living, love, marriage and parenthood,
become distorted right from the start into something
"naughty," "dirty," and downright "nasty."

Why, oh why, is the little baby so darling and cute
when he looks at, and tries out his fingers and toes—
then some months later, he's a beast, a monster, and at
best a pervert if he discovers he has a penis? How could
the poor kid know it was loaded? Loaded with all the
prejudices we bring to it that pay off in our divorce
courts and our broken homes every day?

Most parents who aren't prudish and who keep their
eyes open at all do know that sooner or later little Jimmy
and little Susie discover their genital apparatuses. They
haven't yet been told that it is "naughty" or "dirty" to
play with certain parts of themselves. In various ways,
however, they usually soon learn it. Nevertheless they
develop various methods of "play," and unless they are
awfully cowed they are not going to give up such pleasur-
able satisfactions. Rocking and rolling and jumping give
them some stimulus and pleasure in this area. Manual
manipulation is a common method. The psychiatrists refer
to this as infantile masturbation. In 99 out of 100 cases,
the parent can ignore it on the basis that it is a normal
event and be assured that the child will pass on to more
interesting activities. In those instances where the parent
feels the need to intervene, the best advice is to help the
child to find more interesting play through diversion and
substitution.

If you take the trouble to notice, you'll find that the
child has a very real interest in his or her sexual organs.
This interest extends to those of playmates. Most of
us can remember "show off" or "doctor" parties somewhere back in our childhoods around our fifth, sixth or
seventh years. The differences between the organs of the
sexes and between those of children and adults are mat-

ters of perfectly clean natural human curiosity to children and their interest in these isn't anything for parents to go into a tizzy about.

If a child has his fair share of brains and if you haven't scared him or in some other way forced into him some faulty attitudes that make him feel this whole area of life is taboo, he is going to throw a lot of questions at you along about this time. Where do babies come from? How do they get out? How did they get in? Etc., etc. Many parents duck these questions by shouting—"Oh look! See the pretty bird," or "Daddy's busy now; you go play with your wagon" *but* if they do skip it, the child is going to get his or her answers somewhere else. The odds are that how and where he gets them won't be half as good for him as if he is quietly, calmly, and matter-of-factly told the truth in terms understandable to him—and we don't mean bees, butterflies and flowers—to say nothing of storks, rosebushes and cabbage heads.

A generation ago there were not many sources of such information for parents. So they often evaded answering questions because they didn't know how to do so. Moreover many parents *hoped* that their children would never learn about "sex" until they were ready to be married (and many still do!). Such parents damaged their children in proportion to their own irresponsibility.

The "normal" child needs to be told that *grown up* human beings, both male and female, have important parts to play in producing a baby. The best person in the world to tell him or her this truth is a loved and trusted mother or father.

Except for those who are unusually unobservant or restricted, children witness animals in the act of copulation sooner or later, and if the only explanation they ever get of it is what other boys and girls tell them, they are likely to have some badly distorted ideas about sexual love and parenthood.

If a parent has the attitude that sex is dirty or naughty, he is bound to convey that same attitude to the child. If he is embarrassed in trying to answer questions the child is going to consider this as disapproval. It is unfortunate that so many parents have so much emotional reaction about sex that they won't or can't talk about it. It is surprising to many parents how satisfied a child is with a very simple statement about the reproductive process. And also, that periodically it is necessary for them to answer the same questions again and again, though at a different level of development and eventually in greater detail. If the child is free to discuss the matter with his parents he will often bring home for verification the garbled ideas about sex that he has received from other children. Any real and lasting confusion or distress he feels about this area of interest is most often due to parental conflicts and bungling.

It is not important whether we explain that it is a father's *sperm* or a *seed* that fertilizes the tiny *egg* or *ovum* inside mother that then starts to grow into a baby. That we give *an explanation* when the child is genuinely curious is important. Often the prospect of a coming addition to his own family or the arrival of a litter of puppies makes the explanation a natural and timely one. It is better to grasp the opportunity when he raises the question than to deliver a set, formal lecture with great solemnity and thus over-emphasize it in his thinking. If we use illustrations of animals or birds to make the story clear, we must be sure not to leave the child with the idea that mother always walks around with a load of breakable hen-sized eggs inside her as some children have been led to believe. And, all of this is not difficult if we will say to ourselves, "I have been asked an intelligent question by a human being I love and respect, and I intend to tell him or her the truth before somebody else beats me to it with lies or a garbled half-truth." Then when we start, we can't go very far wrong in fulfilling one of our greatest responsibilities to a child.

Some other important suggestions in giving sex information to a child: Always answer one question at a time and do not flood him with information for which he is not ready. The child's question is a fair indication of his ability and readiness to accept and digest the fact requested. Then too, some parents are inclined to enlighten the child when they (the parents) are inspired to do so rather than waiting for an indication as to when the child is ready for it.

The truth, no matter how clumsily told, will never do as much damage in the long haul as will lies—no matter how fanciful and entertaining the lies may be.

OEDIPUS CONFLICT

One of the early difficulties that is common to all of us in our babyhood is the problem of trying to become oriented to two different persons, mama and papa. It all starts because you and I have to learn about our own respective sexes and their role as we see them in our parents.

This problem of orientation of the boy baby to the two parents is called the Oedipus conflict. It derives its name from the Greek myth of Oedipus who accidentally killed his own father and unknowingly married his own mother. The struggle of a little girl is known as the Electra complex, named after the daughter of Agamemnon who remained devoted and loyal to her father after his death despite the fact that her mother, Clytemnestra, made her into a slave girl.

Our knowledge of how the child orients himself to his parents is based on the observations and study of many years by many, many different psychiatrists. They have verified and amplified Freud's original observations as a result of their detailed examination and treatment of thousands of patients.

Initially, the boy baby is most attached to his mother and continues to be until the third or fourth year. This is not only because she takes care of him, nurses him, gives him his food and is with him much of the time. An important factor in his relation to her is that she is a woman, a female, and he is a male.

During these early years his relationship to his father is unclear to him. To be sure, father is around a little, maybe plays with him a bit (we hope), but he also appears to be a rival who loves the mother and receives some of the mother's love. The little boy sees that his father is much bigger and stronger than he is. He seems to sense a problem in the fact the father is a man and he is a boy, but they are both of the same sex. Furthermore they "love" the same woman. Therefore, the son develops a feeling of competition with his father for the love of his mother. In addition to the feeling of competition there is some actual hostility towards the father. This can be greatly intensified if a father is excessive in his demonstration of affection to his wife in front of the child. On the other hand, the mother can intensify the child's hostility towards the father by her excessive demonstration of affection to her husband. It is this general principle that leads to the very positive advice to parents that they should never have sexual relations in the same room with their child, even when "presumably" he (or she) is asleep, certainly not after the first six months of his life.

The keen parent can often observe some of these expressions of infantile envy and hostility. It is not the well-developed hate of an adult. Up until three or four years of age almost always the child runs to his mother if he is hurt and may even refuse to accept ministrations from father. *After* that time he frequently will run to his father. The little baby, before the age of three or four sometimes is frank enough to express lack of interest when father returns from a trip. He may intrude during demonstrations of affection between the parents.

If parents are reasonably devoted to the baby and they are adjusted to each other, most little boys solve these conflicts without any permanent scars. If a father is a "good" father and expresses his love and affection for him, the child is *aware* of it. The child also perceives that the father approves and wants him to love the mother and the mother to love the child. His conclusion is that the best way out of the problem is to share mother. So he ends the dilemma by joining forces with father and becoming an ally instead of a competitor. In so doing he makes an effort to imitate father and be like him.

Again the astute parent can notice this change. The little boy wants to do things the way father does them, "to be like Daddy." Often this imitation is quite conspicuous around the age of four or five, when the little boy wants to have his room with the same kind of equipment that daddy has in his room. He wants to hang his clothes like daddy hangs his clothes. He wants to have a saw and hammer like daddy has. In an infinite number of ways he indicates this union with Dad, as he makes father his model. This even applies to his standing up at the toilet to urinate because father does instead of sitting down the way mother does, although he *is* interested in why mother doesn't also stand up.

During this period of orientation to his father the small boy also is conscious of a fear that his genitals may not ever grow as large as daddy's or that they may be removed. He has discovered that they can give him pleasure and that his parents disapprove of his taking advantage of them as a source of gratification. Since parents can deprive him of a plaything they do not wish him to have he fears punishment for his enjoyment by castration.

The small boy's conflict is extremely complicated and a statement of its existence is not likely to seem very convincing to the reader when presented in the abbreviated form we must use. Scientific study has given much evidence of its validity. For instance on this last point, the "castration anxiety," as it is called, is a *common* finding in certain types of mental illness. It is linked to the childhood situation in which masturbation was considered as a "sin" for which the natural punishment feared (or sometimes even desired or self-performed!) is removal of the genitals.

Obviously, this is a crucial time for the child and, therefore, for the parents. Difficulties can arise when the mother insists on making the child cling to her or when the father doesn't appreciate or assume his responsibilities towards the baby. The problem really becomes complicated when there isn't any father, through death or divorce or continued absence. The boy doesn't have a model and the chances for his development of masculinity are proportionately decreased. Even the unusually intelligent mother, faced with such a problem, runs a chance that without a father substitute her boy may become a mama's boy or a sissy or at least have too many "feminine" traits or interests. Here's where older brothers, uncles, godfathers, even male friends can play a vital role.

Girls go through similar maneuvers in becoming oriented to their parents but the parental objects, of course, are reversed. The struggle comes in giving up the competition with mother for the love of father. Then the little girl identifies and becomes the ally of her mother to share her father. The process of imitating the parent of the same sex. we call *Identification*. It is really a kind of imitation by means of which the boy, patterning himself after his father, acquires the characteristically masculine traits; the girl in patterning herself after mother acquires feminine traits.

Sometimes the girl can't make an adequate identification with her mother. This may be because the mother rejects her (that may mean anything from a frank ignoring and disliking to an attitude characterized by neglect or lack of expressed affection). Sometimes failure to identify happens when there isn't an adequate mother figure. Sometimes it happens when the father pays undue attention to the little girl child and doesn't give the mother enough, or when he is too busy to bother with either of them. All of these affect the child at the time she is making this new alignment.

There are, of course, lots of boys who acquire an unusual number of feminine traits. There are lots of girls who try very hard, even through their teens to be boys. Even their conscious attitude is that they don't want to be girls. In extreme cases when this wrong identification continues women can't get along with other females. Because they deny much of their own feminine nature, they can't get along with men either except with feminine men who will play a passive role. Some do make brief and passing contacts with masculine men but on a psychologically unhealthy, and therefore unsuccessful basis.

From this struggle we all retain both masculine and feminine traits to a greater or lesser degree. Many career girls have a large element of the masculine in them and husbands with dishpan hands reveal a feminine aspect. Even the curly-haired, petite bits of physical femininity and the hairy-chested stevedores have some characteristics of the opposite sex. For success or failure in becoming like others of our own sex, we can thank or curse the training and influences that shaped our early lives. In the oral stage, when we used to toss off our milk, we weren't caring whether we were going to grow up to crochet or to be the best blocking fullback of Central High. But as adults our relationships are greatly determined by our sexual characteristics. The chances are that if we have grown up with more than "average" admixture of femininity and masculinity, we have probably built up some defenses and explanations that at least satisfy ourselves and protect us from distress about them.

Still one other generality we have to take into account in this very early development of us is that in addition to growing up, there is always the tendency to slip back. It was lots easier to keep sucking on a nipple than to try to manipulate that funny, clumsy cup. Consequently, if we had a choice there isn't any doubt which one we kept on using. It was lots of fun playing in the sand pile and it may have taken pretty nearly a shaming on the part of the rest of the gang before we conceded we were too old for it. We still enjoy sand play on the beach.

One of the parent's chief responsibilities is to help the little child go from one stage of development to the next. This means that the parent must give special support during these changes, whether it is from the bottle to the cup or whether it is from all fours to the first steps on two feet. Let any of us have an accident in those first tries and it may be a long time before we make further effort in that direction on our own. Patience appropriate to the task, well-timed praise and encouragement can do much in childhood not only to prevent us from slipping back but to aid us in going forward on the road from babyhood to adulthood. The parent has to "grow" with the child. He will have to change many of his ways of thinking and acting. He has to decide whether he wants the child to be an independent personality or a dependent facsimile of himself, the parent.

It is also important not to rush the child from one stage of development to the next. He will move along— with a little encouragement—as he is psychologically and physiologically ready to do so. It is a little like climbing a ladder—each rung takes courage; one has to forego a *certain* security with each step upward. It is much easier to stay at a level where you know you are secure and have satisfaction than to climb further. And it is easier to go backwards if the forward step or the present level is frightening.

In this business of growing up, every step makes us take on a little more responsibility, for ourselves and for the world. It is easy to look back and see those carefree days when we didn't have all of our present worries, jobs and responsibilities. Sometimes it is pretty tempting to slip quietly back down that ladder of development to the "good old days."

That is just what lots of people do. That is what all of us do under some circumstances. You will see many adult intelligent people going back to babyhood in a big way when they are physically sick. They get fussy, demanding and even whiny.

For instance, after many of us have put in a hard day and are physically worn out, we may not be that adult, gracious, considerate person we are when we are up to snuff.

The terrifying feature for some people on their first visit to a psychiatric hospital is seeing so many people who have slipped back, sometimes completely to childhood. Also it is distressing for most of us to see the "second childhood" of some old people and know full well that it might come to us.

Slipping back usually occurs when the stress becomes too great for us to bear. It is easy to say that we should avoid situations which cause excess stress. If we *could,* we wouldn't be so likely to have to regress. Certainly we often need to *plan* in order to prevent some stresses. Nevertheless, too often we can't escape some tough conditions and our only preventive of regression is the utilization of all available supports or means of temporary relief. Under the latter heading would fall nature's regular antidote to activity—sleep. For some folk, an extra amount of sleep—rest, relaxation, even vacation—will recharge the personality sufficiently to permit adjustment to the stress. Probably the strongest buttress is the love and confidence of relatives and friends—both spoken and unspoken. As adults we respond to pats on the back just as we did to encouragement and praise as children.

If we find ourselves too often wanting to slip back or actually doing so, then we need professional help. We need such help before we reach the place of those people in psychiatric hospitals, many of whom gave up trying to keep up.

Some people tend to regress a little with advancing years. Usually the persons who have been immature and overly dependent, tend to become more so. By contrast, some people always keep growing—socializing, reading, enjoying hobbies, learning new things—regardless of their age. It is only when we lose interest in the life about us that we regress. Old age doesn't require that to come about, even when crippled with physical infirmities. Thickening of the blood vessels, stiffened joints, more brittle bones, weakened vision may all be handicaps but they don't have to stop one's total enjoyment of life—unless one lets them.

LATENCY PERIOD

Beginning about the age of six or seven or eight, the child gradually enters a sexually latent period. By that time in life little Jimmy and Susie are getting interested in lots of other things and have less interest in parts of their bodies. This doesn't mean that they give up interest

in sex but they just haven't as much time for it as when
they were a little younger and their world was much
smaller. They're going to go on learning things about it—
even out of the gutter. They are unlikely to miss an
opportunity for a little investigative "show-off" party
which may take place in the neighborhood.

The intensity of that interest does diminish, however.
Jimmy or Susie will spend most of his or her interest
on getting gratification out of play and school work. We
can hope that some of their earlier conflicts about sex
have become a little further clarified and the whole subject better understood.

Furthermore, instead of being all wrapped up in themselves, children begin to invest some of their interest in
other people, their pals and schoolmates. At this time
they have their first opportunity to develop real affection
and attachment for companions in their somewhat en-
larged but still small and familiar world—playmates,
teachers, heroes and heroines.

CHAPTER IV

THE DEVELOPMENT OF OUR
RELATIONSHIPS

S THE primitive psychological life urges or drives to obtain gratification and pleasure are expressed by various methods (oral, anal and genital), the human being also learns to direct his energies and interests toward different types of objects (persons) in the seeking of that same gratification

In our development or process of "growing up" to become well-balanced persons, fitted to take our places in human society, we all pass through four evolutionary phases in the investment of interest. Each phase involves a new choice of object to receive that investment.

OBJECTLESS PHASE

The first thing worthy of an infant's interest is himself, or what he thinks is part of himself. From his viewpoint his crib, mother's loving arms and breast or the bottle are merely extensions of him. A healthy little baby is totally self-centered.

This period is referred to as the *Objectless* phase. To the extent that he realizes anything else exists, he regards it as all part of him. He is the center and periphery of his world. H E is all that he cares about.

41

This statement may sound questionable to those mothers and fathers who *know* perfectly well that their baby likes *them* a lot *very* early in life. They are very right in feeling this, for the truth is that at this stage the baby regards them as pleasant parts of himself. Hand him a rubber ball or a spool of thread and if he likes the feel of it he'll try to make it a part of himself by stuffing as much of it into his mouth as he can get there.

His pleasures at that age are the mechanical activity he creates: sucking, biting, squirming, kicking, jumping, doing those entertaining push ups and urinating and defecating. He gets his fun with various parts and extensions of himself. Under ideal conditions such as immediately after feeding or in his bath, any observer can see his delight in physical activity.

The important responsibility for the parents during this phase of development is to recognize the big job that our little baby has in orienting himself to the world and differentiating himself from it and from us. His personality is extremely plastic and sensitive. Even if he doesn't remember it as an adult, he is going to reflect the experiences of this first year. You can be sure that he will show the effect of excessive frustration (those denials of freedom of expression), of the lack of love and affection. The parents can bring him up in a regimented, ritualistic, mechanical fashion or on the other hand, they can introduce him to a friendly, loving and happy world.

NARCISSISTIC PHASE

There is an old Greek myth of Narcissus who fell in love with his own reflection in the pond and because of no response from his image, pined away to his death. That is where the psychiatrists got their name for this second phase of development on Object Finding.

By the time the child is two years old, he has found

out that the world is divided into two parts: himself on one side, and everything else on the other. However, there still isn't a shadow of a doubt for him as to which of those two parts is the more important.

He has discovered that even Mom, Mama, Mummy or Mother is something separate from him, and though he usually gives her a second priority in his affections, his overwhelmingly favorite person is still himself.

But the *narcissistic phase* implies much more for baby than merely being interested in himself. The little child has to learn the rules—the rules his parents have made and the rules that the world has made. In our objectless phase we lived by our own rules, but in this one we have to begin to learn what other people believe and think and say we must do. It's a gradual transition from the time we were entirely on our own to a time when we must accommodate our wishes to those of others around us. But we don't give up easily being the center of the world. In varying degrees we'd like to go on with that same effortless, every-thing-come-to-me life. On this basis it's understandable why we want to attract attention; we want to go on being the center of things just as we used to be. And so it is during this period that we all were terrific show-offs.

We would do practically anything to attract attention: scream, yell, wet our pants, throw things, strut around like an Atlantic City beauty queen, or as a last resort, eat our chopped liver the way someone wanted us to. You have doubtless seen many a mother swoop like a hawk to control her two-year-old daughter who has found out that by pulling her pretty starched pinafore clear up over her head to show her panties she can "wow" the company every time.

Many parents are especially disturbed about that kind of exhibitionism in the presence of little boys, or, if it's the young master who is showing off his parts, they may be fearful of little girls being in the audience. Actually a large part of the parental objection to such behavior is the fear of an accusation against them that they haven't brought up their children properly. They may not appreciate that this is quite a natural and normal and commonplace event. We cannot and should not approve of it but we should not make a great to-do about it.

In the early period when this occurs, it's primarily an effort to attract attention. Children find that certain ways of doing this have a premium and they're quick to learn those. If they aren't too inhibited (i.e., severely squelched and therefore shy and timid) they're going to be ingenious in devising ways of getting the spot light turned on themselves. Sometimes this is accomplished by acting "cute"; sometimes by acting "smart"; sometimes by temper tantrums; sometimes by pouting; sometimes by being very good little boys or girls.

In this narcissistic phase one will notice that unless somebody works hard to the contrary, two-year-olds may mix among themselves on a co-educational basis with no quarter given or asked for difference in sex. But they haven't learned the rules of playing together, in a sense of sharing their play. They may enjoy being around each other, but it makes no difference in their activities whether they wear skirts or pants. If they aren't stopped, boys have just as much fun with dolls as do girls, and girls have just as much fun with guns as do boys. They play with or grab from a playmate regardless of sex.

Billy may be the soul of gallantry to Mary when they are both twenty years old, but when they are two and are put into the same play pen, Billy will have no reluctance in hitting Mary with her own red wagon if she tries to take it away from him. Social responsibility and generosity don't mean a thing to him at that age.

At the age of three or four, this interest in self is at its height, both as to intensity and variety of expression.

It's about at this time that the normal child becomes extremely self-assertive. If mother spanks him there is no reason why he can't spank mother. If spanking follows disobedience, his interpretation of the rule is that it should apply as well when mother disobeys him as to when he disobeys mother. Furthermore he wants a chance to boss at least part of the time. He also wants to avoid being held accountable when he knows he has broken a rule. It is certainly within a normal range to expect the little child of this age to do some lying, perhaps some stealing. In other words the child tries many different methods to gain his ends.

Fortunate is the child who has parents who recognize his behavior as events in "normal" development and handle the situation by teaching which is motivated through affection and not anger, and by explanations that have meaning for the child. To merely announce prohibitions and deal out blanket punishment is storing up trouble for the child and themselves.

As life begins to expand for the child, however, and includes playmates and school teachers, he begins to get an inkling of the property rights of others. He learns that to share something brings love; to take something away from someone brings hate.

He finds out that if he invests some of this love and interest for himself in others, it can still pay dividends in gratification. He learned his first lesson about this back in the anal stage in relation to his parents. Now he begins to experience the results of the same technique applied in many situations.

If mother or teacher, whom he likes, approves and makes him feel good when he lets Mary ride his tricycle, then Billy will learn to swap a ride on his tricycle for that new satisfaction. He is learning to *give* in order to *get*.

We learn to love because our parents love us. We feel

secure because of their love and soon recognize that we are the gainers if we conform to their guidance. This learning to conform is our first way of expressing our love to them. Usually the more we invest the more we receive. In the process of becoming a mature person, our role changes to the opposite position in many respects— from being dependent to becoming independent, from being taught to becoming the teacher, from being protected to becoming the protector, from being the recipient to becoming the donor of love. Psychological maturity implies that one's greatest satisfaction is derived from being the giver of love rather than the receiver (the infantile position). The pay-off of this is that he who gives also receives.

To be sure, some people learn to love even though deprived of it in childhood. But they are the exceptions. Some learn through suffering. Some learn through fortuitous circumstances early in life that give them some kind of an initial substitute source of love.

Religious, moral and ethical persuasions have long taught the necessity of loving. Now psychiatry re-enforces this belief by finding that we have to learn to love others for the sake of our own mental health and peace of mind. If we don't we aren't healthy.

About three-quarters of the patients in the mental hospitals across this country are poor souls who were starved for love in childhood. If they were loved, it was in such a way that they didn't learn to give love in return. Their only recourse was to find satisfaction within themselves. They were forced to remain in or return to that narcissistic stage and build their own world. They have lots of country and city cousins among people outside of hospitals who, because of experiences in early life, were rebuffed, or got too low a rate of interest on their investment. They'd like to love other people and be loved by them, but are afraid to expose themselves to further rejection.

This narcissistic phase is with us in diminishing intensity throughout life. We have to go a long way into maturity to leave behind that three-year-old, to reach a point in our development where we will willingly lay down our lives for the good of others.

There is another little flare-up of our Narcissism when we hit the stretch of life that we call *Puberty* or *Adolescence*. Along about the 12th or 13th to the 16th or 17th years we all experience a renewed interest in this fascinating creature "ME." Along with a concern about "How do I look," goes a normal curiosity and indulgence in the form of self-love that we call masturbation.

This renewed interest in *Self* at adolescence usually fades again to a lesser dominance and we move on in our "growing up." However, we never leave it all behind. And perish the thought that we should. Hold-overs from the narcissism of our early years are the very backbone of some of the greatest virtues of a decent man or woman.

Intelligent pride, self-respect, confidence and interest in ourselves are all properly proportioned forms of "Self-love." It's only in the "sick" or pathological man or woman that too much of it remains as the chief means of gratification.

Narrow mindedness, conceit, and selfishness are as sure signs that we haven't "grown up" as would be our rolling on the floor and sticking our toes in our mouths to get attention.

HOMOSEXUAL PHASE

Homosexual interest is the feeling Willy has for Tommy when those two ten-year-olds would rather shoot marbles together than play dolls with all the local nine-year-old females you could find for them.

It also means what Grandpa feels toward his cronies who sit with him around the club house and swap lies, reminisce and play pitch. What those old boys feel toward each other is separate in their personalities from their interests and relationships with women. And it is also a long way from the popular conception of being "Homosexual."

As used here *Homosexual* applies to a female's interest in and love for other females just as well as to a male's fondness for another male.

We all limited our interest largely to members of the same sex from about the age of ten into early adolescence. Seeking an *Object* (a person) of the same sex in whom to invest love and interest is routine in normal development. This is the age of chums, pals, buddies and the "gang" for boys; "crushes," "very best friends," and "the bunch" or "the crowd" for girls. It's because a normal child at this stage sees something of himself mirrored in those most like himself that organizations like the Scouts, Y.M.C.A., and camps and youth organizations are attractive.

It's an easier transition for pig-tailed Joan to transfer some of her self-love to pig-tailed Dorothy, than to make the whole swing over to big-footed bumptious John, so Girl Scouts, Y.W.C.A. flourish as well as coveys of junior bobby-soxers.

A word here to parents. Children at this age are going to begin to assert their independence—that is if we give them a chance. They are going to want "to belong," whether it is to the gang or the club or the troop or the "bunch." They will be subject very much to the opinions and behavior of their social group. They will begin to protest against the family system if it conflicts with the group system, whether it concerns dress or the hour to come in or other privileges to be permitted. The wise parent has to do some adjusting here along with the child.

Father and mother have to grow too—in tolerance and in understanding. If the child hasn't learned to have confidence in and respect for the parental attitudes and discipline by this age, the chances are he is not going to learn from a continued enforcement of the rules laid down five or even three years previously.

Because of prudishness or ignorance or both, many presumably intelligent parents do not seem to recognize that it is in this stage of development that most children masturbate, sometimes alone, sometimes in a group. This is normal behavior at this stage in life. It does no physical harm. It does no mental harm except in those cases when the child has been made to feel guilty by his own parents who have told him that it was a sin or would drive him insane or would stunt his growth or in some other way damage him. If the child has no fear or anxiety connected with this activity, the parents need not feel concerned. In rare instances, excessive masturbation may be one symptom, along with many other evidences, of maladjustment. Any treatment should be directed at the total problem and not at the one symptom of masturbation. In all cases it *is* a form of self-love, but the great majority of us outgrow this to invest our love and interest in other people and other things.

In our particular culture, the boy at this age has learned most of this sexual information from his pals if he hasn't learned it from his parents. Nevertheless it is very much in order that he be given an opportunity to supplement his knowledge in a very natural uninhibited chat with either of his parents.

In the adult, the carry-over of the satisfaction derived from love for and association with members of the same sex is what gives rise to the development of true friendship, comradeship, patriotism and "love" for mankind in general.

Just because we excluded the opposite sex between the

ages of nine and fourteen, it doesn't follow that "exclusively" men's clubs or women's organizations represented
stunted growth and development. Fraternity and sorority
organizations, lodges, clubs and societies are all "normal"
expressions of gratification which had its beginnings in
childhood relationships. Normal people should and do
carry into later life a capacity for real enjoyment of
pleasures with groups of persons of their own sex as ex-
emplified in the sewing circle or the poker session.

There are a few people who never outgrow this phase
in development. Some are satisfied to carry on merely
sociable, friendly relationships with members of their
own sex but have nothing to do with the other one. There
is another group of persons who, on the surface, make a
heterosexual adjustment; that is, they get interested in and
even marry one of the opposite sex but underneath they
have very strong unconscious inclinations toward physical
love for someone of the same sex This comes to the fore
sometimes under the influence of alcohol even though it
is controlled and consciously denied all of the rest of the
time. Then there are a few who remain in this phase
and their interest in the same sex culminates in gratification through sexual relations. These are the pathological
personalities that most people think of whenever they
use the word "homosexual."

As one commonly hears the word used, it refers only
to an adult who is variously described as "unbalanced,"
"perverted," "criminal," and very often is regarded as
just too low down a form of scum of humanity to talk
about. A surprising number of intelligent people have a
great deal of hostile emotional feeling towards such individuals, berating them, calling them unprintable names
and condemning them with great vehemence. In those
cases, one can almost always be sure that, entirely unknowingly, such persons are defending some latent interest of
their own in that same direction.

This unfortunate adult maladjustment is by no means the only meaning of the word. For the psychiatrist, homosexuality carries none of the popular emotional hostility and it has a far broader meaning than genital activity between adult persons of the same sex. In the technical sense it means interest in and even love for others of the same sex.

Used colloquially love has many different meanings. One loves his wife, his children, his dog, nature and maybe the world at large. And all these loves are different. But they all indicate a fondness for, attachment to, and interest in the object. Except the love for one's mate, none of them imply sexual relations. Neither psychiatrists, nor do we in this book, automatically equate love with sexuality or with genital activity. Love is used in the sense that a child "loves" his parents, or his brother, or his best friend, and it does not imply any conscious sexual interest in the person loved. It is broad enough to include a demonstration of physical affection on the part of an adult son towards his father without reading into it some hidden or unrecognized genital component.

HETEROSEXUAL PHASE

In this private little evolution that each of us experiences, we come at last to the phase where our object choice for our interests and affections is a member of the other sex: "Boy Meets Girl."

The basic urge in this direction is related to the attainment of physical maturity. Also, no longer do previous attachments completely meet the psychological needs. Our interest shifts to members of the opposite sex in the beginning search for a final and permanent type of an object for our major emotional investment.

We give to this new object of interest the sensuality of infancy and the tenderness we acquired when we first learned to love our parents, teachers, and friends. Another faint wave of Narcissism is likely to wash over us, as we "spruce up" in order to be attractive to this new object that we have discovered.

This is the phase in our development that often is rough for the adoring parents and it's known to be rough for the adolescent as well. The psychological as well as the physical changes that take place are so radical that even in the best adjusted families, it is likely that there will be some tears for mother, some extra bills for father, and some periods of revolt for the son or daughter. The striving toward a new love object entails a straining away from old ones.

Physiologic changes take place in preparation for or as a part of this development which are worthy of a word of comment. There are some mothers who do not seem to know that their sons, beginning at the ages of 12 or 13 are likely to have nocturnal emissions—"wet dreams"—that occur during their sleep. These are perfectly normal occurrences which the boy should be told to expect. When they do occur they best be ignored. If anything is said about them, it should be in a reassuring and understanding matter-of-fact way. Too often when the lad does not understand them, he becomes anxious and upset on the assumption that they are related to, if not the result of masturbation. To him they may appear as evidence that he has "harmed" himself.

The second point is that in this age period the average girl begins to menstruate. We need to make no great fuss, flurry or ceremony about this normal natural event. It is extremely important that the little girl should be told that it is going to come and what to expect before there is any question of its beginning. This warning, however, doesn't need to be couched in terms of alarm or a threat or a "curse." It ought to be explained in simple, natural and understandable language—what to expect, what it means, and what to do about it. If the parent doesn't know what the daughter knows about her sexual apparatus and reproduction, it is a good opportunity to find out and to supplement her knowledge. If such knowledge is intelligently given it will certainly stand her in good stead in the heterosexual adjustment that will occur within a year or two.

This sexual education should certainly go far enough to explain the principles of sexual relations, not only so that the girl might have a clear understanding but also to insure correction of mistaken ideas. For instance, it is a surprising fact that there are even college girls who have the naive assumption that one can become pregnant by being kissed.

Unfortunately, some young people are never able to make this shift of interest to a member of the opposite sex on their own. So they may never reach this heterosexual stage for the reason that as males they cannot accept the role of masculinity or as females the role of femininity with all the attendant responsibilities and obligations.

There is no rule of thumb as to how to anticipate or avoid such difficulties. One can't say even that there is a specific age when these general changes take place. Sometimes it is as early as twelve; sometimes it is as late as eighteen. All things being equal and the rest of the life adjustments satisfactory, no one needs to have any great worry about its earliness or tardiness.

Sometimes the young man or woman will stay shy of the opposite sex until relatively late in the teens. This may or may not be symptomatic of other difficulties. Apparent disinterest may serve as a means of self-protection against insecurity, insecurity as to whether they will be liked or wanted or know how to act. Sometimes either sex may do a lot of casting around with short attachments here or there or on the other hand remain serious with the "first love."

Parents should regard this transition as a transforma-
tion from childhood to adulthood. Once the change starts
it takes place at a rapid speed, accompanied by many
symptoms of revolt and hypersensitiveness. Young people
are very often justified in their feeling that their parents
haven't recognized that they have grown up. If the apron
strings are held too tightly, there will be defiance whether
it is about what clothes to wear, or the hour to come
in after a date, or the use of the family car.

In playing the new role of adulthood they try to be
very sure that no one mistakes them for children. In the
boy we see the pretenses at great masculinity. In the girl
we see an intensification of those things she regards as
special feminine attributes—personal attractiveness, co-
quettishness, demureness, and often a relatively sudden
easy familiarity around members of the opposite sex.

In both young men and women we find an even
stronger adherence to the group opinion and the group
methods than during the homosexual stage. The necessity
to conform often distresses parents. The young folks over-
evaluate the wisdom of their judgment, failing to recognize their lack of experience or their limited abilities.
This applies equally to their opinion of the amount of
sleep they need or the way they drive the car. There
are, too, many real and fancied causes of unhappiness and
disappointment that occur frequently within this stage
of development—failure to be chosen by the fraternity,
not being asked for dates to a special party, becoming
a nonentity in the university after being a high school
"big shot."

Lots of these difficulties have recently been blamed on
the "mom." There isn't any doubt that in many instances,
mom keeps the apron strings too tight. When she over-
protects and forces her attention and her opinions and
her decisions on the growing child, it may be because
father doesn't assume his share of the parental partner

ship. Mom shouldn't have to carry the entire burden of rearing a family. It's equally father's responsibility, and if father ignores it or neglects it or refuses to accept it, it is hardly fair to incriminate just Mom.

Psychiatrists do not have any simple short bits of advice about this age for parents. The problems are too numerous and too diverse to be covered by any generalities. The parental aim has to be the same as that of their children, namely to help the young son or the young daughter develop his or her independence and gradual emancipation from the childhood home. This implies that the parents have to continue to adjust in their attitudes towards and their management of their relationships with their adolescent offspring. It *is* hard for some parents to let their children grow up. It is hard for all of us to recognize that they *do* grow up. If we as parents grow with them, we can help them; if we fail to grow with them, we hinder them. The cutting of the child's attachment to the parents and the dependence on their authority is a mutual job.

The adult person who has reached and accepted the heterosexual stage of adjustment successfully has, under ordinary circumstances, developed certain characteristic relationships with the opposite sex. This individual:

feels at ease with himself or herself,
when with a person of the opposite sex finds satisfaction in such company,
is not fearful of the opposite sex,
is not a "woman-hater" or a "man-hater,"
has outgrown childhood attitudes of regarding a person of the opposite sex as an alternate mother or father.

Satisfactory heterosexual adjustment is essential to a happy marriage. In fact many of the marriages that go on the rocks do so because the participants either never reached this stage of development or didn't adjust to it. Sometimes for purely narcissistic reasons they selected for a mate someone too like themselves. Too frequently the man unconsciously sought and found a substitute for his mother, or the girl for her father. Conceivably, such marriages can work out happily; they may meet the unrecognized psychological needs of both persons; perhaps even more often both parties to the bargain help each other orient and develop further psychologically. Sometimes one or both find it necessary to seek professional assistance in their struggle to make the union hold.

Successful marriage also implies sexual adjustment on the part of both parties. Unfortunately this too often is not the case. Many couples who, to the external world, seem to be well adjusted and regard themselves as happily married reveal to the psychiatrist that the wife is not sexually adjusted. Through the ignorance or selfishness of the husband or the shyness of the wife or both, the wife never achieves the satisfaction of a climax to sexual intercourse—an orgasm. Often neither partner knows that she should! Then in addition to ignorance about the techniques of making love, there may be the inhibiting force of a fear of pregnancy. Another restraining force is the strong indoctrination of girls in childhood of the attitude that sex is naughty and dirty, which point of view is maintained later by their "protected" lives. Too many wives, intelligent ones too, believe that sexual relations are part of their "marital duty"; that they must give their husbands satisfaction, even though they feel that it is not "nice" for them to have comparable pleasure.

The capacity for or desire to have sexual relations with a member of the opposite sex is not a criterion of adequate heterosexual adjustment. In fact, such activity may be an indication of a lower level of psychological adjustment as is usually the case with those men and women who *have* to "have" numerous affairs. Even when sexual relations between a couple are mutually satis-factory, this fact alone is no proof of matured hetero-sexual adjustment nor evidence that a marriage between them would be a happy one. Sexual compatibility is necessary to successful marriage but it does not insure it.

In or out of marriage, an individual can learn to find satisfaction in channelling the energy of his sexual drive into creative, socially approved outlets. These outlets may be far removed from sexuality. One can make a good social adjustment, i.e., be happy and comfortable with members of the opposite sex, without participation in sexual intercourse.

AMBIVALENCE

The growing-up process, including the changing of ob-ject choices in which we invest our interest, is compli-cated by another factor that we've ignored up to this point. That factor is the conflict between our conscious opinion or attitude and our unconscious opinion or atti-tude. They often don't agree but we are usually quite unaware of that disagreement. This conflict is very im-portant when these contrary attitudes are expressed in our relationships with other people. But the origin of this ever-present influence in our relationships goes back to the very beginning of our development.

As small children, in fact as babies, we have to start making choices. That means we have to make decisions. Literally we very early have to learn whether we are going to have our cake or whether we are going to eat it. Probably the first big decision or choice comes in the toilet training period. Will the baby have a bowel move-ment and thus win praise and love from mother, or will he hold on and find his pleasure in asserting his own wishes to her displeasure? One of the solutions of this problem that some people learn when they are very young is to go through the motions of doing what is expected but in some degree having their own way too. We can play at our job; we can stall; we can do it grudgingly— and poorly; we can do it and exact a premium; we can "goldbrick" or "soldier."

This business of trying to say yes *and* no to the same question is one that troubles a lot of us all through life. Partly because the learning of this lesson was started so early, we even fool ourselves. A part of us says yes and a part of us says no. It gets pretty complicated when the "yes" part of us happens to be our conscious thoughts and wishes and the "no" part of us is unconscious. But that often happens. That division of opinion within us is often quite transparent to other people. It is rarely evident to the victim of that conflict.

Everybody knows Jim makes such an ado about loving his wife. He talks about his affection for her and he carries her picture with him all the time. He sends her flowers and candy and brings her jewelry. The fact is, however, he never can remember their wedding date or her birthday. He seems to find much to do down at the club four nights a week with the other boys. If he does break down and go to a dance because his wife wants him to, he spends most of the evening with the other ladies and lets her shift for herself. He makes it necessary for her to ask him for every cent that she gets, for the grocery bill, the bill for Jimmy's shoes and her lipstick. If there is something she wants done around the house he always finds himself too busy to do anything about it. He really thinks he loves her, but everybody else can see that his is a pretty confused kind of love.

There are lots of us who have traits somewhat similar to Jim's. We think we really want to do something but somehow or other we never get around to doing it. We know we ought to go call on the Smiths and the Joneses, but we just *have* to go to see that picture that is only at the movie this one evening. We do love our two little boys very much and we know that we want to help them build that playhouse they have been talking about. Some how or other we just don't get to it.

All of us in various ways indicate that we have double attitudes and opinions about various things. We swear that we only have one but a good look by anyone who can watch us in action sees another one. This yes-no behavior is termed *Ambivalence*. Like chemical elements, ideas and emotions may have different values or valences, different weights, different interpretations. We can be ambivalent towards our job or our religion, towards our civic responsibility or our avocation, our friends or our relatives.

ADDITIONAL ENVIRONMENTAL FACTORS

At this point we need to fill in a gap in the record. The infantile and childhood training and the choices the personality makes of various persons in which to invest interest at various stages is not nearly all of the story of how we grow up. This internal development produces the internal "works" but the human being doesn't function in a vacuum. What he is is a combination of what goes on inside of him *plus* what goes on *around* him. Life is always an interaction between what and where we are.

We grow up in a particular social structure and in a particular type of culture. The child in Samoa and the child in Akron start out with the same kind of physical stuff but the social scene in which they live has a great deal to do with the differences in the way they look at and react to life.

The family structure also has a lot to do with the way our characters form. In America, family life shows wide variations in standards, attitudes, methods. Children show an equally wide variation. But, theoretically at least, we still subscribe to the family ideal of a father and mother who have joint responsibilities, who work together as a team with an appropriate division of the labor and the fun of bringing up a family.

Even within the family there are differences in personality patterns. The only child, the oldest, middle and the youngest, each develop their own characteristic variations. The members of a small family have a point of view and course in life which is different from that of a very large family. It makes a lot of difference in attitudes whether the economic status of the family is high or low during childhood.

The personality will show the effects of culture, in the form of travel, musical opportunities or extensive reading. Another varying factor is the educational experience, whether it is in one of the large municipal schools or in a one-teacher rural school. The social structure influences us through the presence or absence of its many organizations, gangs, clubs, Scouts; by life in a teeming city or on an isolated farm or in a small rural community. The church is a vital part of the American scene. For many of us religious experiences played an influential role in the shaping of our personality. The fact that we have the privilege of growing up in this particular democracy contributes very much to what we are as persons.

There are at least three connecting links between the family and social structure, and the personality of the individual growing up in them. These are automatic psychological devices that have a lot to do with making us the way we are.

The first of these is a process that the psychiatrists call *Introjection.* It is the automatic absorption into one's self of the emotional attitudes, the wishes, objectives and ideals of other persons or groups of persons.

By this means we actually get something from others

or the environment and build it into our own personalities. We "eat" it up—with our eyes or ears so that it becomes a part of us. Or, we can live with it until it is a part of us. "It gets in our blood"—or "under our skin"—or "We take it into our hearts."

We will see later on that one of the most important parts of our personality, our conscience, consist of ideals and attitudes that we take over mostly from our parents and install into ourselves, very early in life. But we introject much more than our consciences—our behavior towards people, our sense of values, our ideas. It is a little disconcerting to recognize that most of what we are we have gotten from someone else.

When we look at a baby—which all of us were—we know that he hasn't much "personality." He has to absorb it from his environment. From the time that he can manipulate his hands, he usually begins to incorporate things, including his nipple, his rubber ball, and his ideas. Some go into his mouth and some into his mind. This type of behavior is characteristic of all of us, all the rest of our lives. We introject—food, ideas, opinions, prejudices, love.

We do this every day, every hour, every minute. Transient jobs of Introjection are quite automatic. We go to a party and feel gay and happy because it is a good party. We are really taking in the "spirit of the party" and in a way setting it into motion in ourselves.

This incorporation of the spirit of a crowd or mob can be on some occasions a healthy and fruitful exhibition of Introjection. "Let's all pitch in and help this man get his house built."

But taking into ourselves the spirit of a mob that starts off with, "Let's all go kill that so-and-so" who maybe did or didn't do something we didn't like, is a wild pathological disease of humanity that demonstrates introjection in its worst form.

In addition to Introjection which builds so much into our lives, another personality device which is important in helping us belong to a group is *Identification*. We discussed this mechanism briefly as an important aid to the child in his solution of the Oedipus conflict.

We always use Identification in relation to other people. It is another automatic process by which we put ourselves into another person's shoes and take over for (or with) him. As long as the situation exists or permits, we assume the attributes or aims of someone else or several other people for whom or towards whom we feel a strong positive attachment. This can happen without any deliberate intent, very often even without our recognition of what is going on. We imitate other people because we respect and admire (identify with) them. Mothers know all about it. They have been known to say: "Thank heavens the Lone Ranger rides around doing good."

Much of our behavior that many people think of as the product of heredity is really the result of Identification and Introjection. How many times we say that, "He is just like his father" or "She is just like her mother." What we are often talking about is mannerisms, gestures and ways of doing things that the child saw in his parents and unconsciously imitated for the rest of his life.

Identification operating in children is very apparent. We do not recognize it so readily in adults. The little boy "apes" his father consciously and unconsciously. In his play, he acts the part of an Indian Brave or a G-Man or a General. He is identifying with his hero.

Mothers of little girls would do well to look into the behavior mirror that is furnished for them by their daughters at play. How Sally talks to her doll, how she loves and takes care of dollie or doesn't, is sometimes very revealing to the mother who can recognize the reflection of herself.

The theater and the movies are excellent laboratories

in which to watch Identification in process, as the audience has a good cry or a good laugh when the hero or heroine cries or laughs.

What mothers or fathers, or whoever feeds the baby, haven't caught themselves opening their own mouths like little baby birds every time they pushed a spoonful of Pablum or chopped carrots at their offsprings' faces?

And if you never shoved the fellow next to you nearly off his seat in the stadium as *you* carried the ball for your Alma Mater from the two-yard line to the touch-down—you just don't have all of your machinery with which to make Identifications.

It is the power to identify with the group that leads to the development of teamwork. The stronger the Identification with the group, the more individualism each person in the group loses willingly. The group aims and standards and purposes all become property of every individual member. It was and is one of the strongest supports against stress for the personality in the B-29 team, the football team, the sales squad, the ready-to-wear department, the sixth grade at Polk School, the old Troop 2, the family. It is the process by which each of us is able to feel that he belongs.

There is one rather common kick-back that often comes out of Identification, and that is a tendency on the part of some people to *assume*—or presume—the powers, or virtues, or ability of others and then to feel "superior" themselves.

There were the paratroopers, for instance, who just because they were paratroopers assumed that they were the equal of any five ordinary men. Maybe they were. Then there are those people who, because they collect a crooner's records and swoon when they are played, look with disdain and pathos on the efforts of the amateur barbershop quartette. Because we try to hang onto the coat tail of the great or near-great doesn't give us their abilities, even if we sometimes assume it does. In such instances our Identification, mixed with bad judgment and immaturity, leads us to make fools of ourselves.

The third automatic device that helps us in developing our personality in relation to other people is a short-cutting device that lets one thing stand for something else. We call it *Symbolization*.

We are all familiar with the many examples of the purely conscious symbols that play such an important role in our daily lives. Words, for instance, are merely symbols. Symbolization is operating when we salute the flag, wear wedding rings, notice the small golden eagle on a veteran's coat. The piece of cloth or the lumps of metal on an Army uniform take on meanings through associations that give them emotional value. If a man loves his country, the people in it and the idealism for which they stand, you would do well not to jump up and down on the colored piece of silk or cotton that is his flag, at least in his presence. Literature, particularly mythology and fairy tales, and art employ symbols to represent related ideas.

The use of Symbolization as a mental mechanism however is unconscious. We use symbols unconsciously, just the same way as we do consciously, but for valid psychological reasons, we don't know we are using them nor even that they are symbols. The symbol is acceptable or meaningless or unrecognized as such but it is used because the idea or object for which it stands would be totally unacceptable to the conscious self. The mechanism becomes more complicated because a conscious symbol may have an unconscious meaning, either directly or through associated ideas. For instance the May pole dance had its origin in a spring ceremonial connected with flowers, fresh young trees and sexual indulgence. Were it not for its factual historical evolution, one might be accused of having a "dirty" mind to suggest such an idea. Symbolization frequently occurs in our relationships with certain types of persons: the nurse often quite unconsciously is regarded as a mother figure by her patient; one may like all policemen because they represent protection or hate all of them because they represent demanding authority.

Another mixture or combination of conscious and unconscious Symbolization was quite evident in the Army. The wearers of symbols of rank and authority in the military world, insignia, were often all dumped into a common heap in many a G-I's thinking and called "brass." This was in a way conscious Symbolizing. Not many G-I's recognized the unconscious Symbolization that was going on at the same time when they reacted toward their officers as they might toward their fathers.

Those who enforce governmental, school or any other external authority are really symbols of earlier law-enforcers. Our attitudes toward *any* authority were largely shaped by our parents. The boy who quarrels with and resents authority through school, college and in his work as well as in the Army or Navy is still unconsciously reacting to paternal demand.

Many buck privates hated the sight of any lieutenant (good or bad—there were both). If you asked one of them what he thought of his dad he would probably insist that he had always "loved" him. However, if you learned to know him a little better you might find that he often resented his dad. The chances are that you'd never get him to admit his deepest feeling, namely that he really deeply hated or feared his father. He never could admit his unconscious childhood resentment because he just didn't recognize it as such. Nor did he understand that his resistance to all authority was his reaction to a father-symbol.

Our dreams are filled with examples of Symbolization in which objects and people are representing others.

We're all familiar with the harmless and unimportant little fears of specific things. For instance lots of people have an inordinate fear of snakes. More irrational is the fear of mice, bugs, spiders, and bats. The only adequate explanation of such fears is that they do have some kind of unconscious symbolic significance. It doesn't make much difference what the symbolism is in these cases because first, the fear isn't very important. Second, even if one does know what the symbol is it doesn't necessarily change the emotional pressure in the unconscious.

For many of us, the sight of a piece of yellow paper in the hands of a messenger boy can produce a "gone" feeling at the pit of the stomach because of both conscious and unconscious Symbolization.

How we react to grey hair on old ladies has little to do with the stuff that they brush and comb, but more with what those ladies represent to us because the dynamism of Symbolization is functioning.

These three devices, *Introjection, Identification, Symbolization,* play a major role in making us what we are. They tie us to the world we live in. They are all automatic processes which tend to make us one with the family and the society into which we were born.

PSYCHOLOGICAL MATURITY

Before leaving the discussion of the stages of development and environmental influences, we should make an attempt to describe that ideal state, psychological maturity. The experiences of the infant—feeding, toilet training and genital curiosity—are the basis of his patterns of relating himself to the people around him. As he grows older, he changes his investment of interest from himself exclusively to include other people. As we have tried to indicate, growing-up always takes place in a particular social structure and in a particular type of culture which also affects the formation of life patterns. The variations in the economic, intellectual, social and cultural levels of the family influence the end-result of personality development.

Psychological maturity is an ideal state. It is questionable if any considerable number of psychiatrists would characterize it in the same way. They would agree probably that few people reach the ideal. Those who do, deviate from it frequently. One might postulate that reaching psychological maturity implies successful passage through all the infantile and childhood developmental stages without crippling events which might cause the storing-up of deep-seated conflicts of major proportions.

In positive terms, we can state that psychological maturity entails finding greater satisfaction in giving than in receiving (the reversal of the infantile state); having a capacity to form satisfying and permanent loyalties; being primarily a creative, contributing person; having learned to profit from experience; having a freedom from fear (anxiety) with a resulting true serenity and not a psuedo absence of tension; and accepting and making the most of unchangeable reality when it confronts one.

We have said that psychological maturity was an ideal state and that few reached it. On the other hand it would be a serious error not to indicate that many if not most people can approach it. No matter what the psychological injuries of infancy or childhood may have been, they rarely if ever are insurmountable barriers to reaching a state of near-maturity. As we become less selfish, less prejudiced, or more considerate, more creative, more generous, more cooperative, more intelligent, etc.—we become more mature. The only hope for the future is that more persons will approach closer to maturity, and that the next generation has a much higher average level of maturity than we, the present generation.

CHAPTER V

THE STRUGGLE

A HASTY GLANCE at the last week, the last month or the last year leaves little doubt that life for most of us is a struggle. There are a thousand and one little struggles within the big struggle—making that nipple work on the baby's bottle, getting the washing done, writing that long overdue letter, squeezing out some money from the budget to buy those extra clothes. Then there are always the more serious ones that occur in the lives of everyone—the baby gets sick, the misunderstandings among the family or with friends, the economic emergencies, depressions, even wars. The sum total of all these make up the bigger struggle, that of getting along happily and profitably with our family and our friends and our associates, in short in making a life.

The point psychiatry makes is that all of us make the struggle much easier or much harder for ourselves depending on how our personalities function.

So often we think we know just why we do a certain thing or why we feel a certain way. Once in a long while we aren't quite so sure why we think so or why we feel so. Psychiatrists tell us that many of our ideas and many of our emotions have a motive which is beyond our own conscious recognition.

The theory is, as we have said in the first chapter, that

68

there is one part of us that seems to be under our voluntary control and a larger part which is *not* under our voluntary control. It's not exactly a Doctor Jekyll and Mr. Hyde act, because one part isn't necessarily bad and the other good; it's more like one of these clown acts in a two-part fake horse with the man up front trying to make the whole thing seem to behave while he never knows what the guy back underneath the rear end is going to do next.

The strange part of the individual that is so unpredictable and irrational is called the *Unconscious* for want of a better name to pin on something nobody has been able to explain otherwise.

The way we use the term, it's a large region of the mind that the conscious part of us can't get at by any ordinary ways of questioning or thinking about it. More about this will come later, but meanwhile:

The Unconscious part of us and the *Conscious,* together make up what is called our *Personality.* It's the sum total of all we have been, are now, and hope to be; it's our minds, bodies, memories, habits, abilities, faults, experiences; it's us from our hair-dos to the way we keep our tempers. In short, in your case it's what other people think and talk about when they mean YOU.

That Personality is affected by its contact with everything else outside itself: friends, enemies, jobs, homes, noisy steam pipes, automobiles, whooping cough, pneumonia, high school dramatics, jet propelled planes, the high cost of living, etc., all of which we put, for convenience, under the heading, *Environment.*

When Personality meets up with Environment, as ours did the day we were born, something has to give, no matter whether we succeed in making life a bed of roses or a never-ending rat-race. For the rest of our life we have to make adjustments to and of our Environment or we just don't live. It's that simple.

In this struggle for adjustment some of the Personality is continuously changing and so is Environment.

In the morning, cheerily whistling, we may be chiefly concerned with getting the toaster to work at breakfast. By afternoon we may be gloomily wondering whether we can get a job in San Francisco if the boss fires us as he said he would when we stayed out to lunch an extra half hour. Every situation is different and we conduct ourselves differently and react quite differently in each.

Day in and day out, hour by hour, in fact minute by minute, the Personality and the Environment are colliding, and the outcome of each of these collisions is either success (adjustment) or failure (maladjustment) in varying degrees.

Most of us have witnessed the differences in the reactions of Personalities to onslaughts from Environment. Some can take the total loss of their homes and fortunes; they adjust to the death of loved ones or maiming handicaps. Others can't. Not many Personalities can still be in there adjusting after a full speed head-on collision with as solid a piece of Environment as a ten-ton truck.

Our failures are expressed in one of two types of reaction—Flight or Attack. If we come up against a situation that is too much for us to take in our stride, to accept or manage, (and it doesn't knock us out as said truck would) we dodge it or run away from it or we try to kick the stuffing out of it, one way or another.

In a Flight reaction the Personality usually suffers directly—as in sickness, drunkenness, loss of standing or prestige. How much, depends on the demands made on it by the Environment and the strength of the Personality to meet these. All of us have seen the flight reactions of pouting, sulking, irritability, or deep depressions. There was a time not so long ago when it was a good ten to one bet that a "lady" would swoon away if the language or the "going" got too rough. Swooning and fainting, either for real cause or in hopes of landing in a movie hero's arms, is a Flight reaction that is guaranteed to get one out of a situation, even if it is only temporary. In pouting or passing out, the Personality is running away from an Environment it can't accept or manage. What's more, all our Personalities resort to Flight, at one time or another.

All our Personalities also certainly have used the Attack reaction to some situations that we didn't like. Who hasn't reached the point where he just lashed out at Environment to change it or destroy it?

The six-year-old who takes the living room apart like a cyclone because he can't have a lollipop ten minutes before supper, and the man who wrecks his business career because he feels he must poke his boss in the nose for something he said, are both Personalities having Attack reactions.

After failure to adjust, be it by Flight or Attack, there is always the possibility of readjustment, i.e. compromise or recovery.

Fortunately most of our failures are minor ones, and readjustment is fairly simple. Sometimes we merely need a little more sleep at nights, other times we only need to use more intelligence and less emotion. Many times we can call on help to relieve our burden of activity. Ideally the solution is always a matter of compromise: The Personality gives a little and the Environment gives a little.

Occasionally our failures are too great for us to recover from without assistance. Our maladjustment to bacteria may send us to the hospital. The sixteen-year-old down the street may land in court for having tried to destroy his allowance troubles by robbing the hardware store. Others we know have "nervous breakdowns," divorces, take to solitary drinking and so on down the line.

Frequently, someone can help: the doctor, the clergy-man, the parent, teacher, social worker or good friend

Finding a good listener is all that we need at times. We can blow off steam to him. Often he can give us a little understanding, advice or sympathy, sometimes, medicine. Often he can help us change the environment or suggest changes in it, at least enough to straighten things out. But the world can be pushed around just so much. Certainly the larger share of relief in most cases must come through changes that we make in ourselves—new understanding, a different attitude or approach or more rest, or perhaps recreation.

There is a continuing need for each of us to have some understanding of why we as particular Personalities react in a particular way to a particular environment. Straightening out serious maladjustments is no job for an amateur, but most of us can use to advantage some understanding of the factors operating in our make-up that help determine the outcome of our daily struggle.

Whether we, that is our conscious and our unconscious parts, decide to take Flight or to Fight is determined by a lot of things. By and large, when the going gets too tough, most of us react in a fairly consistent fashion. Because of the nature of our development some of us are too aggressive and ready to fight while some of us are too passive and weak-kneed.

One of the biggest determinants in our choice of Flight or Fight reaction is the stuff that we are made of. By this we mean the capabilities and the potentialities of the germ plasms that we got from our parents and that they got from their parents. Some wise man said, "You can't make a silk purse out of a sow's ear." Most of us hope we have a little better endowment than that, but for better or for worse we are limited by the same principle.

Our training and experience in infancy and childhood is by all odds the most important factor in determining our course of action. Our early lives established patterns of reactions in all of us, patterns that we use, regardless of what the problem is or what the environment is.

The type of reaction varies in all of us, however, depending on the strength or the weakness of our personality at the moment. Even if our general pattern is to take Flight or to Fight, if we are tired out, our response is certainly modified. If we go without sleep for four nights or stay on a bat for four days, the chances are that in either case, the regular patterns of reaction will be changed.

Finally, the Flight-Fight responses depend somewhat on the nature of the situation to which we react. In growing up we all had real conflicts, some of which we solved, in a poor way. The fact is, even if it was a bad way, that's the way *we* learned to solve that type of problem. As adults, we may go on using that same poor solution for the same general type of conflict. If we could look at anybody's personality with a microscope, we would find some poorly or partially solved conflicts that sometimes, under pressure, turn out to be Achilles' heels. Especially is that true when the pressure—i.e., the problem— in some way is similar to that which led to a poor solution way back in childhood.

In everyday life, we all make minor Flight and Fight responses, depending upon how we feel and upon how much is demanded of us. Most of the time we make our little failures, learn from them and do better. Usually, we make constructive compromises.

The whole process of growth, training and education is one of learning how to make these constructive compromises. We have to modify what we want with what we can get. We have to modify what we do with what is demanded of us.

If we fail badly; that is, have very marked excursions into Flight or Fight, the results are called symptoms. On the other hand, most of us most of the time avoid that by a device that the personality has developed which is technically called *Sublimation.* This is the method that we use day in and day out, probably more than any other in order to keep ourselves living and liking it.

Sublimation is the method by which our primitive urges and instincts and impulses that demand gratification find outlets in ways that pipe off this energy into actions and activities that are acceptable to the outside world and often are highly useful.

The personality really has to sublimate nearly all of those primitive aggressive and erotic interests that spring from the depths of the personality and keep demanding expression. We do directly express and satisfy our needs of hunger, sexual wants and eliminative processes. But most of our normal, healthy actions and behavior represent various types of Sublimation. We learn to do this quite naturally in the business of growing up. As infants, we started with certain interests and methods of gratifying those interests. Then we periodically reached a stage of growth when we had to give up a particular method of gaining gratification and develop a new one, and maybe even to find a new but related interest. Again and again, as we developed, we had "to put away childish things" in favor of more adult outlets and methods. Each step was a modification of and a substitution for the previous step. At each stage we made further progress in adjusting instinctive needs to adult social codes and demands. The adult personality then is the result of an evolutional process in which the original interests and methods have in most instances become deflected very far from the starting point.

Perhaps an example will help clarify the point. The baby, somehow, in his first year discovers the fun of smearing his own excrement all over the surrounding territory as well as himself. It must have been fun if one is to judge by his effectiveness. But he soon "learned" that that just wasn't done.

Within his first three years, he, like all of us who had a chance, found real sport in playing with mud, as mud pies or making and throwing balls of it, or even in just playing in it. (Note here the nigh universal tendency to pick up wet snow, make a ball of it and throw it—usually at some one! But it isn't "dirty.") Understandably, most mothers do not approve of mud playing as a pastime, and so diverted us to the dehydrated product in the sand pile. Even there we sometimes slipped back to the hydrated stage by wetting it down a bit so it would stick together. To make an even more solid product we added shells or pebbles, or stones or brick. Maybe we began to collect some of them and maybe they became special treasures. We started building roads, houses, tunnels, bridges. From there it was a short step to the manipulation of toy automobiles and airplanes that made play life so much more real; and then to erector sets, electric trains, toy soldier battles, and elaborate constructive activity.

Sublimation is a learning process in which without really recognizing all the reasons, we gave up old interests for related new ones; we even forgot and disclaimed satisfaction from those former interests—we totally repressed the original aim. When we can find ways of expressing the aggressive drive in constructive ways we sublimate it and therefore do not have to express it by being mean, hateful or destructive. When we do considerate or thoughtful or generous things for our family or friends, we are sublimating the energy which in its original expression would have been purely erotic (sexual).

One's capacity to sublimate—to convert primitive energy to socially worth-while endeavors unconsciously (automatically)—is some indication of his state of mental health. In general it is true that the greater that capacity, the better is one's mental health, and conversely, this is also true. The seriously mentally ill person just doesn't sublimate at all.

Consequently, the more sources of real satisfaction that one can find, the more mentally healthy he can be. If a person regularly has some satisfying outlets—Sublimations—they undoubtedly help keep him in a healthier state of mind. For that reason avocations are eminently worthwhile. Whittling wooden ducks, making ship models or doll houses, painting the kitchen, working in the garden, arranging the stamp collection, clipping the hedge, knocking the golf ball, writing a book, puttering at something constructive—these along with a thousand like actions are all compromises—Sublimations—that convert our primitive energy into socially approved activity.

Punching a bag, socking a baseball, and pasting a little white ball so that it goes 200 yards down the fairway, or facing the man on the other side of a tennis net, are all acceptable ways of releasing tensions—sublimating—that might otherwise be turned loose in an attack reaction on wife, children, boss, cop, dog, or—you name it.

For many of us our jobs are routine. There often isn't much chance for individual expression or initiative—and usually lots of opportunity for frustration. And yet all of us need—if we stay mentally healthy—a liberal share of personal satisfaction. Hobbies can fill that need: We can choose them, we can putter or play with them in just the way it suits us; we can get real gratification out of our acquisitions, our "work," our skill. So they serve, not only as Sublimations but as anchors of interest and satisfaction to the windward in the time of emotional storm.

It is a wise and fortunate individual who was sublimating when he chose his job. Just as the teacher and nurse derive gratification and release from tension in their work with children, so, many other occupations present opportunities to direct basically primitive energies along profitable and constructive channels.

Most of us carry shreds of childish pleasure in cruelty and in the infliction of pain, even if we can't admit it. Fortunately, we have many constructive outlets in pruning, trimming, cutting, trapping, hunting. It's very possible that there is some Sublimation for this for the student in the dissecting laboratory or even for the butcher in his work. Perhaps its ultimate refinement is seen in the skilled work of the surgeon while busy at the task of saving lives. There are some doctors, who in their earnest effort to help, twist your sprained ankle three times, apparently wanting confirmation for a third time that his manipulation hurt!

How many bankers will heave this book across the room and into the fire at the suggestion that they too are sublimating in their calling? To many of them it will be inconceivable that their toilet training and the infant gratification they experienced in power, dominance, independence and collecting foreshadowed the pattern of their needs that are filled by their occupation today.

The power of prejudice against the discussion of such possibilities is often so great that Sublimation of the anger aroused is necessary in order to lower the blood pressure of the reader.

In one way or another we keep on sublimating unless we give up trying to behave like adult human beings. Then we resort to an attack or a flight. When we sublimate we keep ourselves well; when we attack or take flight too often or too far, we are not well.

PERSONALITY STRUCTURE

THE FOLLOWING explanation of the personality structure is based on a theory held by many psychiatrists. It deals with the factors that mainly determine why we behave the way we do. The personality is terrifically complex. There are general patterns of human behavior. In different people these may, however, show important minor differences. Unrecognized causes produce their effects, long forgotten experiences and training have certain results, parental actions lead to unexpected child reactions. One can explain the operation of an automobile by a demonstration of the working of its various parts. We can see the relationship between the spark plugs and the carburetor, the transmission to the differential. But we can't explain much about human behavior by the closest investigation of the physical parts. We could take man apart and lay the pieces on a table, and still couldn't begin to explain his actions.

In some ways the psychoanalytic theory of personality structure is as difficult to explain as the atomic theory. A top flight nuclear physicist may try to demonstrate with little tinker-toy arrangements what really happens among atoms, nucleii, neutrons, protons, etc. They can't simplify the real thing any more than Rube Goldberg can, but they can and did do this: they found that so and so happened under such and such conditions. They believed that if this and that were done thus and so might result. The first explosion at Alamogardo Air Base that rocked us into a new and fearful age proved that at least some of their theory was and is correct.

The men and women who have devoted their lives to trying honestly to find out what makes us do what we do, have advanced many theories.

This is one of them that has grown out of the thinking and experience of Freud and many other people. One of the things we have to keep straight in this discussion is that the word personality doesn't mean what Hollywood and Success Courses have made us think of when the term is used.

As pointed out in last chapter the psychiatrist uses the term personality to mean the individual *as a whole,* the sum total of his characteristics and reactions, both physical and psychological. It's his body as well as his mind, plus the responses of every part of the body, the thinking (intellectual) and the feeling (emotional) make-up. It's the working as well as the works.

So many "parts" we talk about are to be thought of as *forces* operating through related units rather than any chunks of material we can separate from the rest.

One way to picture the personality structure is to think of it in terms of three levels: *Consciousness, Unconsciousness* and between these a sort of mezzanine or border territory called *Fore-consciousness.*

If we talked in terms of light, we could liken *Consciousness* to full daylight; it is closest to the surface and in nearest contact with the outside world. This is the major storehouse where we keep our working knowledge. It is where we do our "thinking"; it registers what we see and feel and hear and do. It is what we think ourselves to be.

Below this Conscious zone and gradually fading away

without any sharp boundary lines, is the twilight zone of
the Fore-conscious. This area is sort of a crossing over territory. Ideas we forget, either by intent or disuse, pass
through or are stored temporarily at this level. Names,
events, ideas fade as they slide into the twilight of the
Fore-conscious. Sometimes these can be recalled easily;
sometimes we have a hard time bringing them back, no
matter how we work at it. Eventually they may slip or
are pushed into the darkness or "night" of that lower
level we call the Unconscious.

The Unconscious is the cellar of the personality. We
know of its presence by the supply of energy that keeps
coming from the drives originating there. Into it go the
taboo memories of experiences, colored by our emotional
reactions to them. Its only contact with the world is that
which the Conscious permits. Yet we cannot by conscious
effort reach down into it.

A pretty good way to demonstrate what these three
zones amount to in terms of our daily experiences would
be to ask ourselves three types of questions.

"How old are you?" (Or any other inquiry about your
present status.)

You know the answer right off. It's right up there on
the top level of Consciousness.

The second type of question has to do with old memories, things we might ordinarily assume we know but
just have no occasion to recall. For instance, "What is the
name of that kid who lived just down the street from me
who was such a bully? I knew him *too* well when I was
ten years old!"

"No, it wasn't Harley—Hartford?—no, Harrisburg—no,
that's a city in Pennsylvania. Hargrave?—Holtsman?—
Hancock?"

Well, it may come to us from our Fore-conscious level,
but if we are like most people we might just as well stop
trying to remember it right now. The Personality just

blocks faster than we can dig, particularly if we thoroughly disliked him anyway and were glad when his family moved away.

At least we have a "feeling" for the name and we know we knew it very well at one time. A lot of memories fall in this same area through disuse—how to find cube root, those Latin poems, and the name of the capital of the Belgian Congo.

The last type of question is harder to pose. It would have to do with experiences that happened to us but that we cannot recall at all. A lot of our experiences that happened one or thirty years ago were so mild or bland or unimportant that they completely slipped from our memory. It has been shown, however, that actually none of these is forgotten entirely.

In contrast to those that sort of "slipped" from our memory, are those experiences, ideas and thoughts that were surrounded with so much emotion that they were forced out. The emotion apparently disappeared along with the memory. In fact, it was the emotional surcharge that had a lot to do with the enforced "forgetting." Some of those experiences were important in shaping our personalities.

To indicate what we mean, we cannot recall when we gave up our mother's nipple or the nursing bottle; or our feelings when our next younger brother or sister arrived in the world and we were sort of shelved. We do not remember when we *first* became curious about sex differences, what provoked the curiosity, and what happened about it; nor how we felt when Auntie brought sister a much nicer doll than she brought us.

We might as well give up trying for the answers to this type of question. They are really down in the darkest dark of the deepest layer of our personalities. We can't get at them by any ordinary means of contact, but that doesn't mean that the answers aren't still there.

Scientific study has proved that no important experience is ever entirely forgotten. We can go further and say that no memory is ever completely lost.

The theory of the Unconscious is one of the concepts of analytic psychiatry that has been garbled, misinterpreted, fought over, and often indignantly rejected by skeptics, but it is the keystone of the whole personality structure and as such needs considerable attention.

How do we know there even *is* such a thing as the Unconscious? Where's the proof?

That is a tough assignment for the "experts" when they can't lay the pieces right out there and label them Exhibits A, B, and C. The Unconscious can't be demonstrated like a brain or a set of muscles, nor can it be proved mathematically. *But* there is a lot of evidence in our daily lives which points to the existence of a part of the personality that is not controlled by our conscious wishes and desires.

One experience that is so commonplace that most of us are inclined to pooh-pooh it as evidence of anything, unless we sit down and honestly give it some thought, is what we call "slips of speech" or "slips of the tongue." We fully intend to say one thing, and what comes out is something else again. There are very few of us who haven't done this at one time or another when it proved to be embarrassing.

There is the old story of the polite mother who spent most of the morning coaching her children not to make impolite remarks about the big nose of the visitor who was coming and when he did appear, introduced him as "Mr. Nose."

More than one romance has taken a jolt when "Dearest" in a moment of tenderness was called Marie or Joseph when "Dearest's" name happened to be Jennifer or Thomas.

"Slips" happen to the most careful of us, and if we are honest with ourselves about them, we have to catalogue them somewhere other than under conscious thinking. In fact the embarrassing ones frequently seem to have caught our censor of the personality off guard and jumped out to say just the *opposite* of what we intended.

"Slips" aren't with us only in speech.

Professors aren't the only ones who do the things we call absent-minded.

What cigarette smoker has never put a pencil or something else into his mouth and started to light it?

Did you ever take half your clothes off when all you really went upstairs to do was to change your tie or stockings?

Have you ever gone home and found yourself blocks, maybe miles out of your way, back at the house or apartment you haven't lived in for months, perhaps years?

Did you ever start to ring the door bell at your own home?

Have you ever tried to open your home door with the office key, that isn't even in the same bunch as the one you wanted?

Or, looked for your glasses when they were on you or in your hand?

Where do these "slips" get their push that sends them out?

Even the most skeptical has to admit that their expression indicates that two attitudes towards the same thing must exist. Ordinarily the Conscious is in control. Obviously, it has lapses. When it does the "other half" of the idea which is just lying in wait under emotional pressure, is ready to pop out. Consequently, when it does come out it certainly indicates that there is some other part of the personality that is right there ready to take over. For working purposes, we call it the Unconscious.

Where, if not to the Unconscious, do the experiences of childhood go? Only under unusual circumstances does an adult recall any particular impressions, relationships or clear-cut memories of what went on before his fifth or sixth year.

All of us have a few memory pictures that stay with us down the years, some quite vivid to us, but even they are spotty and often tangled up in the story about them that was repeated and repeated throughout childhood.

Most of the facts of our childhood, however, are forgotten—as to how we learned to be honest or kind or thoughtful, or how we learned to have temper tantrums, to be impatient, or to prefer to be alone. Actually the most formative years of our lives when the main patterns of our future behavior were being set up, between birth and the age of six or seven, are to virtually all of us now a blank. Those memories have faded from our conscious recognition, though they are still very, very much with us and without our knowing it, influence our lives today.

Those powerful memories too have gone below to help make up that part of our personality called our Unconscious.

Coming closer to our today though, where, oh where are the telephone numbers we knew only last week? Or, the name of the man we met at lunch with Jones when we ate the clams that bothered us for two days? Or, for that matter what is the name of that cereal the kids wanted you to buy so they can send the box tops in for a new bicycle? Some things like that are still with us on the top level, but most of it is going or gone to somewhere. Where? According to the theory, they pass into the level of our twilight Fore-conscious, and some of them eventually are catalogued in the subterranean reaches of our Unconscious.

Most of these simple little everyday forgettings aren't

very important. Lots of facts and knowledge slip from recapture by any conscious efforts because of disuse.

However, those ideas or experiences surcharged with emotion in our lives that become conflicts for us don't just "slip" out of the Conscious merely because we don't use them. They are really *shoved* down into the Unconscious. The significant thing is that even though they are forcefully pushed out of the Conscious, they still try to escape back to it. They don't lose their surcharge of emotion and it is the power of this emotional surcharge around the conflict that keeps it a potential trouble maker. This is a process called *Repression* that we will discuss in detail later.

There is also evidence that some "thinking" goes on below the Conscious level. Did you ever have the experience of being all snarled up in a problem, the answer to which escaped you? The more you worried it, fought it and stewed over it, the further away seemed all hope of solution.

Then did you give up in exasperation? Leave it alone, and think you had shoved it aside completely for a while, probably even gone to sleep on it. Then later, perhaps the next morning, Wham! There's your answer, as simple and clear as a crystal!

This can happen to "How to pay off the mortgage" as readily as "How to do Lucy's algebra for her" when you thought you couldn't remember that X ever had a square, to say nothing of a cube root. How does anyone explain that, if we reject the theory that there is an unconscious mental activity?

The child or the adult who walks and talks in his sleep will assure you that the conscious part of his personality doesn't put him into the situations in which he finds himself every now and then at about three o'clock in the morning.

Dreams are additional evidence of an Unconscious.

Nearly everyone dreams at times and most of us look. on our dreams as nonsensical and meaningless mental meanderings which are forgotten on waking. Nevertheless, they are thought processes which are creations of the particular individual. Even though we may not understand the whys and wherefores of them we can't deny them out of existence, nor can we help but realize that they must have some relationship to other thought processes that go on in our minds.

From that region we call the Unconscious, we all derive our life energy. Sometimes this is referred to as instincts or drives. First, last and always, we must never underestimate the power that resides in the Unconscious. It is a dynamic area in the make-up of every one of us and we can't rightly think of it as a limp collection of old discarded experiences or associations.

THE ID, EGO AND SUPER-EGO NETWORK

We think of and have tried to picture the Unconscious and the Conscious as regions or areas, with the Fore-conscious in between. Scattered over these three regions is a functional network of operations that does not entirely coincide with them geographically. This network is split into three parts that in scientific language are referred to as the *Id*, the *Ego* and the *Super-Ego*. The *Id* is the source of instinctual energy, the *Ego* includes all that is our conscious self and the *Super-Ego* is the censor and critic. They are conceived of in terms of dynamic forces that are continually fighting amongst themselves for control of the power that comes from one of them, the Id.

The entire network of the Id is limited to the region of the Unconscious. Most of the Ego is in the Conscious but it covers a portion of the Unconscious. Similarly the Super-Ego is partly Conscious, but much of it is Unconscious.

THE ID

The Id is the source of the two energy drives in any human being: the impulses to Love and to Hate. We can call these drives by a lot of names, but under any title they are still the mainsprings in our movements, young or old, man or woman, Chinese or American. Technically, they are termed the *erotic* and *aggressive* drives. In their most primitive forms—and that means animal-like expressions—one is the seeking for gratification that is primarily sexual; the other is aggressive and destructive. (As we said before, when the psychoanalysts say "sexual," they mean far more than merely genital. The erotic drive as expressed in its primitive forms includes all types of physical gratification. The energy, called the Libido, derived from this primitive drive, is invested initially so that it brings us only physical gratification. As we grow up, it is invested in lots of other ways that bring gratification that are in no sense, except through evolution, related to physical gratification.)

The whole business of life is concerned with the taming and controlling and directing of these two major sources of energy. Either can be expressed in primitive form— erotic play or intense hate. The primitive sexual drive eventually becomes love, constructiveness, tenderness. The aggressive drive emerges as ambition, initiative and push. The energy from either of these drives can become too powerful or can be misdirected. Most of our personality difficulties arise when we don't get a proper fusion and therefore neutralization of them; when one, therefore, gets out of balance with the other.

One of the quickest, easiest ways to catch a glimpse of these two drives getting out of control is to settle down in a comfortable bar.

Alcohol taken in excess, as well as some illnesses, can

weaken the conscious "normal" control of one's behavior. If you stick around long enough, you will see the customers start to exhibit the forces that are pushing up through the cellar floors of their personalities. Some announce themselves as the friends of all the world, or the greatest lovers of all time, and are more than anxious to prove it. Others will start out just arguing about the color of somebody's tie which they don't like, and wind up taking on anybody within two hundred pounds of their fighting weight, or breaking all the bottles or chairs in the joint.

Our Id hasn't any sense of time whatever; it doesn't ever grow up. Its powerful forces continue to demand expression from birth till death and seek it in every possible form. At five or fifty years of age, those yens and demandings are essentially the same and they don't have any use for logic. Just as the tiny baby goes along on the principle of seeking pleasure and gratification in every form that he can find it, and avoiding all the pain and frustration, so does the Id operate all through our lives. It is cut off from the world of reality by the Ego. It is the Ego which has to take on the responsibilities, while Pan-like Id pays no attention to what anybody thinks or cares. It just lets fly. If Ego wants to dress Id's wishes up so they won't be upsetting and shocking to it or to the outside world of neighbors, that's Ego's problem, not Id's.

The Id doesn't speak words, nor does it attempt to express itself in ideas—it just works through forces, through power directed towards the doing of what it wants to do—getting pleasure. Always "it wants."

Id * means "it," and the reason even scientists call

---

* Historically *Id* is a translation of the German *das Es*, borrowed by Freud from Groddeck, who took it from Nietzche.

this region of the Unconscious the "it" is primarily because it is so childish in its behavior that we are ashamed of it and do not want to claim it as any part of us. Actually the calling of this part of our Unconscious "it" is very much like a mother saying, *"It is* grumpy, today," when speaking about her child to another adult, if Junior ("it") happens to be sulking right there in the same room and looking for trouble.

This Id of ours stays infantile and primitive and continuously strives for expression. We truly have a difficult job controlling it and thus always appearing as civilized mature adults. The fact is that none of us are always completely successful.

At three years Id might say, if it verbalized a wish, "I want that cookie right now." At thirty years, "I want that blonde even if she has a husband." At eighty years Id might say in its silent way, "I want quiet around here" and the Id part of grandpa could strangle his beloved grandchildren to get that quiet. The sum total of Grandpa would never let such happen, but this doesn't change the urge from Id. That Id never grows up is sometimes spectacularly demonstrated in an eighty-year-older who wants cookie, blonde, and quiet.

It's fairly easy to see from a few samples of "pure" Id in action that we would get into trouble mighty fast, if Id was all there was to our make-up.

Let's focus our interest for a while on

EGO

This part of our structure we can all feel a little more at home with, because in this breakdown of *Us, Ego* is the network that has a function we are aware of: Ego says, "I will," or "I will not." Ego is the portion of us that has to make the decisions.

Ego knows about environment: what other people will think, what will happen if we butt our heads against a stone wall or a law made by society.

Ego knows that too many cookies lead to stomach aches.

Ego knows that taking that blonde to Mexico just "isn't done" without complications setting in.

And strangling noisy grandchildren is not accepted by society or loving grandfathers.

Ego knows all of this and a lot more and therefore, Ego has to try every waking second to take care of those impulses and demands which irresponsible Id keeps throwing at him and about which he has to keep on making decisions. Can I do this? Can I do that? Without its kicking back on me?

In other words, Ego makes up the bulk of the personality which we ordinarily call Consciousness.

Most of Ego is conscious and it represents the thinking, knowing and feeling part of a person. All that we know and remember is included in this part of us.

While we can't talk about size in trying to picture these circuits, networks, of Ego and Super-Ego, in a way we can think of them growing as we grow, or perhaps it would be better to consider them as getting stronger.

Ego begins to develop at birth and as we learn from experience, its strength and power increase. The first time we learn that a flame is hot and hurts, something has been added to our make-up. It is Ego that records for us what happened on that play: finger touches pretty red and yellow light and finger gets hurt—Okay, now Ego knows. The next time Id tries to get finger to go touch another red and yellow light (Id never learns—or changes—and will just keep on wanting what it wants and sending up impulses, no matter what happens) Ego has learned—maybe. Certainly by the time Ego has had several experiments Baby doesn't need Mother around to grab him and say,

"No, no, no." Ego takes over for her and part of Baby, himself, does the job.

Baby may not weigh an ounce more after he's learned this lesson, but something grew or strengthened inside him as a result of this newly added experience. In this theory of personality structure, that something is what we call Ego.

What goes for Baby goes for adults too. The Id of a forty-year-old may set up impulses to eat a whole roast duck at one sitting, or to kick the sulky, uppity new laundress into the Bendix, but Ego knows what would happen to his digestion and her best linen tablecloth if Id were allowed its way. So Ego probably settles for a wing and just a bit of the stuffing, and leaves the house on wash days.

In addition to this function of consciously controlling and redirecting crude and primitive desires, Ego performs *some* unconscious activities.

Some of the powerful yens, impulses and urges that originate in the Id get sat on and shoved back by Ego into the dark unconscious of Id when Ego *represses* them without our conscious knowledge of the process. The conscious Ego often refuses to recognize Id's desire and even denies its very existence. Then the unconscious part of Ego automatically pushes or holds it down below consciousness without our knowing anything about it. When the unconscious part of Ego won't accept and thus prevents the expression of an urge, a desire, or an impulse, either from the Id or from forgotten lockers in the Ego's own unconscious area, we call the process *Repression*. The conscious part of Ego doesn't know anything about the whole business.

By contrast, when we are aware that we consciously sit on one of these urges or impulses, Ego can be said to *suppress* it, and the process is labelled *Suppression*. In simplest terms, Suppression is a conscious mental action (we are aware of doing it). Repression is an unconscious mental action (we don't know we are doing it).

When we don't eat the whole roast duck and we don't kick the laundress, even though part of our personality wants to, what goes on is Suppression.

It may help to give some illustrations of Repression. They are more complicated than the Suppressions because in Suppression the main factors are fairly clear and apparent, day by day. In Repression a lot of the contributing forces, experiences, and ingredients were put together in us a long time ago and social pressures, taboos and customs force us to try to hide a lot even from ourselves. But what we try to hide continues to seek opportunities for expression and remains down in the unconscious as a source of conflict—"I want"—but "I can't."

To demonstrate, let's take a young father—any young father—and have a look at his relationship to his first born.

Society, his pals at the office, his wife's friends, you, we, everybody he knows is going to regard him as strange or peculiar if he doesn't love that cute new baby and be proud as Punch about it. What is a lot more important is that *he* would look on himself as some kind of a rat lower than anything we could call him, if *he* didn't feel that way about this new creature.

So much for what *we* demand that he feel and what *he* demands that he feel.

But how does he really feel?

If he is a human being like the rest of us, he is going to have, along with his impulses to love, protect, and cherish this son or daughter of his, impulses to resent, envy, be jealous of—and we might as well say it—actually hate that creature. While his wife is suffering in labor he sometimes gets preview flashes of those feelings.

Like any of us who manage to get along fairly well in

the world, his love impulses and reactions to this object will outweigh and be more powerful than the hate ones, but there is no use fooling ourselves into believing that they aren't there. This is a classic example of the ambivalence that we talked about earlier.

Suppose that pretty wife of his brought a Pekinese pup home from the hospital with her, installed it in the bedroom with them, fussed and fretted over it, spent three-quarters of the day and night feeding it, making it comfortable and going to look every time it gave a burp or let out a whimper. How long do you think the husband would go without having any impulses to toss the pup out the second story window?

This baby isn't the same kind of competition as the dog would be but it *is* competition and there is a *part* of the personality of that young father-husband that isn't going to see this situation as anything but blocking and interference with what he wants.

The jealousy, the destructive hate impulses get rejected so fast by the Ego of that father that he may not be aware that they ever existed. All his training and his knowledge of the outside world and reality, what other people would think and feel, just won't let such urges get a hearing up in the conscious level. They are held down in the unconscious so tenaciously with this lightning speed play of Repression that Daddy would say we were liars if we said any part of him ever for one instant hated his "Pride and Joy." For all his conscious personality knows, he is telling the absolute truth.

If all the hatred that the young father actually *unconsciously* experienced towards his baby became conscious, Daddy would be sick with anxiety and his mental balance would be endangered.

Repression, as one of the Ego's defense measures, is a valuable tool. In fact it serves a necessary role in the lives of all of us. It is one of the factors that permits us to really enjoy many of our happiest relationships. In every close friendship between two people there is ambivalence. That is, each one has negative as well as positive feelings toward the other. Only through Repression can we very largely exclude from our conscious recognition one or the other aspects of that ambivalence.

Take for example a couple who believe that they love each other very much. They avow their mutual affection any time the subject comes up, in public or in private. They are not being hypocrites in any sense or faking their feelings. They believe they love each other very deeply. However, this doesn't prevent their ambivalence from occasionally expressing itself. At times they irritate or annoy each other. Almost surely they frustrate each other in some degree. As long as they get enough satisfaction from each other, they will continue to repress, for the most part, any recognition of the hostile feeling for the other one. Consequently Repression operates to permit them to love each other in such a way as to bring with it true happiness in marriage.

Repression can go on for awhile even after the satisfaction between them grows thinner. If he honestly finds that he consistently has a better time out on the golf links or at the ball game than with his wife—or if she always enjoys herself at the Tuesday night bridge session or at a Saturday matinee with Muriel more than when she is with her husband, sooner or later the other aspect of the ambivalence, the hostility, will make itself more and more apparent. It won't be repressed. Just let him double cross her or let her double cross him and all at once love completely turns into consuming hate.

The main point here is that it is a blessing that Repression does operate because it keeps us healthy and well-balanced.

But Repression fails sometimes because of the amount or type of material that we have to repress. It can fail when our Egos become weakened and can't keep the material repressed. People with pretty rough childhoods filled with taboos, prohibitions and restrictions, had to tuck away in their unconscious a lot of impulses powerfully surcharged with emotion that keep trying to gain expression.

Then when the strength of the Ego is depleted, the power of the repressed material may overwhelm it and escape. Or the Ego may become worn down through great external pressure. Sudden shock like the unexpected coming of death or disaster to loved ones may upset Ego's equilibrium and its balance of control.

Whatever the cause, when the Ego fails in its repressing function and some previously repressed material threatens to gain expression, the Ego feels anxious. That usually leads to the development of symptoms.

Even when we go to sleep Ego is still censoring our nighttime thought processes. That's why our mental activities express themselves in the weird and distorted forms that we call dreams.

This job of censorship of dreams which the Ego uses is one of its numerous devices to defend itself against the expression of repressed material. The Ego has to protect itself against the superior power of the Id. Therefore, even though we sleep, its censor is on the job.

The basis of most, if not all, dreams is wish fulfillment. "Wishes" represent desires or yens or urges or inclinations to think or act in a particular way. We dream what the conscious Ego won't let us think when we are awake. In order even to permit some wishes to be expressed in dreams the censor distorts them so grossly that we can't even read their meaning. Even with one of these silly dream interpretation books our dreams don't make any sense because the book wasn't written specifically for us. Falling from a high building, if Jimmy dreams it, means something specifically for Jimmy that has no significance whatever for his mother. Furthermore, the dream is usually illogical and, as everybody knows, very often primitive. In short, dreams always represent wishes which the conscious does not want to accept and to all intents and purposes will not recognize. Once in a long while the little child has a very simple direct wish expression that we can understand. He wants to go to the circus. Mother said he couldn't, so he dreams it. But for most of us as adults, dreams are productions of the unconscious part of the mind which, however, are so censored and disguised that they may with safety come into the conscious part of the personality.

Dreams are useful very frequently to the physician in the process of psychological treatment. They have been described as the Royal Road to the Unconscious. This simply means that because they are excretions from the unconscious, with sufficient objective knowledge and analysis, they may reveal some of the unconscious wishes which the Ego can't see.

Some dreams are terrifying. In fact, the soldier who had endured combat often had such terrifying dreams that he was afraid to go to sleep. The dreams became symptoms, evidences of an Ego in an acute struggle with environment, as do sleep walking and nightmares under less acute stress.

And finally before we leave the discussion of the Ego we should mention its function of controlling all of our voluntary motor activity. It makes the machinery go or stop when we walk, talk, drive a car or pilot a plane.

Unfortunately, there aren't any simple instructions which can be directed to the person whose Ego is having difficulty in censoring or in repressing. The chances are he couldn't use instructions even if they were all written out for him. He needs professional help.

It may be helpful, however, to know that in some degree all of us can, in our healthy states, recognize some of the factors that do support the Ego and thus help it in its job of Repression. We have tried to point out that when the Ego strength is diminished, when it is weakened from any cause, it can't do its job so effectively. Therefore, some suggestions are in order as to how to help maintain the Ego strength. First must come the recognition of the simple fact that the Ego *does need support* or it *will get weak.* Second, we should know the signs of weakening. Often even the recognition of the existence of a problem is a considerable part of its solution.

A simple and often effective support for those who have been under prolonged pressure or stress is rest and relaxation. Sometimes this implies the necessity of getting out of the struggle for a little while. Often it may mean taking a long-postponed vacation. Everyone who knows anything about mental health recognizes periodic vacations as desirable. Sometimes it merely means some extra sleep; sometimes it means some other kind of a change that one can make in his environment.

Another support for the Ego is approval. We all want it and must find ways of getting it from those who count in our lives. This, however, is usually a two-way need. Not only do we need it for ourselves but we have to recognize that other people need it and, therefore, give it. An awareness of lack of approval may indicate that some changes should be made in our attitudes or our methods. Maybe it means some extra work; maybe it means some specific types of work, in line with attitudes or activity of the person or persons from whom we want approval.

Still another support to help our Egos function is the achievement of satisfaction. We have to include sources of satisfaction in our method of living. If we aren't getting it one place then we have to get it in another. If we don't get it from one person then we have to get it from others. Conceivably, this means a change sometimes in our

friends or our job, our playtime, or even our family relationships. Very often it means that we need to invest
some of our energy in hobbies or sports or educational
effort which are shared with family and friends.

A final suggestion as to how to support the Ego is to
have a goal, some objects and some purposes in life. Obviously, we need some immediate and some future ones.
What is it we are looking for? Where are we trying to go?
We each have to sit down wherever we are and think these
out. Now and then we must revise them. Maybe they are
stated in terms of personal ambition, either along vocational or avocational lines. For most of us they can, in
part, be formulated in terms of the family. For lots of us
they are in terms of our immediate job. We all need,
however, some destination and some assurance that we
are on the road that is travelling in that direction.

THE SUPER-EGO

The *Super-Ego,* the third network system of the personality, is the censor and critic. Most of it is unconscious but a little of it is conscious and as such functions
as our conscience.

We don't have any Ego or any Super-Ego when we are
born. They both grow along as we grow. The Super-Ego
starts to develop about the third or fourth year to aid in
the solution of the problem of establishing our relations
towards father, a man, and mother, a woman.

Through babyhood and into childhood, parental do's
and don'ts form the standards of behavior. They are our
total authority, law givers and enforcement agents. As
little children we gradually take over the standards of
our parents and make them a part of our own personalities. This is accomplished by the process of introjection
discussed in an earlier chapter. As we begin to borrow

strength from father and mother by identifying with them, imitating them, trying to be like them, we set up police or censor forces within ourselves—our Super-Egos.

Throughout life, the job of the Super-Ego is to say, "You must *not.*" Sometimes it may seem to say "you must." Actually it says "You *must not* do as you want to do, therefore you *must* do thus and so."

Now everyone of us has a conscience of some dimension which is the conscious representative of the Super-Ego. Because it starts to form so early in life (and gets pretty well along by the eighth to tenth years) the chief models that it copies are naturally the parents and early teachers. Also, however, it is greatly influenced by other factors. For many people religious training and experience were particularly important in laying the foundation of their concepts of right and wrong. The rules and prohibitions which the Super-Ego accepts and builds into its framework are largely forgotten in later life but nonetheless still serve to control our behavior.

If we, "normal" people, play a mean trick on a friend, our consciences make our Egos feel guilty and we need to seek punishment to absolve that guilt. We are usually quite conscious of this sense of guilt and feel as though we ought to do something to square things up again. One example of this is the woman who doesn't invite a friend to a luncheon party when she feels she should because she thinks the friend just wouldn't fit in. Well, like as not, the hostess will go around feeling guilty for a couple of days and wind up by taking the injured party all her best petunias or something like that to do penance.

Often our Super-Egos will force us to make exaggerated efforts to pay for our misdeeds out of all proportion to any damage we might have done anybody. The punishment meted out to Ego doesn't always "fit the crime" when it is Super-Ego that is doing the punishing. Super-Ego is likely to lay it on a little heavy.

The practice of confession in certain religious faiths is one way of relieving and perhaps strengthening the conscience. Some people derive similar benefit from "thinking it through" on their own or confiding in a member of the family or a friend. But for a psychiatric orientation, keep in mind that these methods touch only the conscious part of the Super-Ego.

An unconscious part of the Super-Ego works in the same way as the conscious except that we do not know that it is in operation. Sometimes we can guess that it is functioning because we feel depressed or tense and cannot figure out how to account for those feelings.

We retain only a few conscious memories of life before the age of five. If we lived with our parents long after that, we are probably aware that many of their habits of conduct and behavior are also present in ourselves. We both consciously and unconsciously imitate them in living by their standards. Lots of us as grown folks stop at a moment of decision to consider, "What would mother think?" The Super-Ego was just about set for life by the time we were eight or ten, and if we had never seen our parents again, our Super-Ego would operate today mainly by the set of standards they gave us long ago.

If anyone had the misfortune to have as parents two hard, sour, cheerless people who made childhood a string of unending "don'ts" for everything that was pleasant, that poor unfortunate victim would probably have a Super-Ego that would not allow him to have a good time without suffering for it.

Fortunately, however, Super-Egos are not built with cement and it is possible for them to be re-shaped and modified under favorable conditions. Unless this were so, change in our standards and behavior would be impossible without great stress. Sometimes, as adults, our consciences are too rigid for comfortable living. Their governing rules taken from the parental patterns were cut to fit a different world.

Though difficult and sometimes painful, Super-Ego can be "softened up" a bit to fit the times. This may happen in various ways through education and experience in our daily lives. Sometimes it is the result of the "education" that we receive through our friends. Sometimes it is a part of the re-education of parents by their children. We often hear the remark that "times have changed," i.e. many of us have "liberalized" our attitudes towards certain types of behavior such as smoking or dancing, as well as other previously fixed standards or attitudes. Often in psychiatric treatment, one of the chief jobs is to relax the excessive severity of the Super-Ego.

The Super-Ego is the critic that sits on the sidelines watching hard-working Ego handling the hot ones that Id is forever passing to it. When Ego tries to let some of these strivings and primitive demands of Id go out into the world in some form of action or behavior that Super-Ego doesn't approve of, then poor old Ego suffers for it. Super-Ego criticizes and condemns Ego until it's enough sometimes to make us sick. That's exactly what it does do to us every once in a while.

It is the unconscious part of this bit of our machinery that causes some of our most difficult psychological jams. Sometimes the Super-Ego takes the Ego to task for fancied crimes or sins when the Ego really didn't know it had done anything wrong. In fact, it had not done anything wrong, except in not being able to control impulses from the Id. A man of forty-five in a severe (psychotic) and deep depression, because of his sense of great unworthiness and sinfulness, gave as his explanation of his depression, "I stole 25¢ from my father's pocketbook when I was eight years old." This theft thirty-seven years previously was the only explanation that his conscious personality could give. Psychiatric examination revealed without question that the cause of his depression was related to his unconscious Super-Ego's criticism of a very deeply buried hostility of which he was not consciously aware.

This patient's problem presents another psychological principle: the explanation as given by the Ego of the "cause" of the personality distress is at most only a clue to the real conflict; often there may be no apparent connection. The individual not only has no recognition of the true problem, but is "protected" from seeing it by his psychologic machinery. He creates a smoke screen in the form of some trivial or minor event to which he ascribes great importance.

This particular example illustrates another point, namely that guilt is always associated with hostility. In very simple language, one never finds a sense of guilt that is not related, indirectly or directly, to hostile feelings or hostile acts. We say indirectly because one can feel guilty about a sexual impulse or act that in itself is not hostile. The guilt arises because we defy our own conscience or what somebody else believes about us. In either case that defiance often can be traced back to our parents and their ideals or to our early religious training (our Super-Ego). Consequently the defiance is indirectly a hostile act towards those persons in our early lives as well as those in the current scene whom we "wrong" or disappoint. Then we feel guilty because of the direct expression of hostile feelings or acts. If we behave selfishly or if we've done a dirty trick or even had such a desire, whether conscious or unconscious, we may have that feeling we call *Guilt*.

The Super-Ego always knows when one of those repressed, that is tabooed, ideas escape from the Id in a disguised form. The Ego may not have seen it going past for what it really was, but the Super-Ego did and invariably applies its old horsewhip of criticism and condemnation to the Ego.

Many of the things that the Ego does in response to the criticism of the Super-Ego are worthy and worthwhile. Sometimes the Super-Ego makes us work harder. That is why lots of us just have to do certain things and in just a certain way. And why some of us are super-conscientious. That is why lots of us are over-punctilious and why some of us are over-cleanly. None of us knows really *why* we are that way—if we are. We just know we have to be that way.

Sometimes the Super-Ego can be bribed too, very much as one's conscious conscience can be bribed. Drives to "do good," to up-lift, may be methods of neutralizing one's unconscious forbidden wishes. If we take that friend our best petunias, at least we feel better. We haven't changed the original idea nor even righted the wrong; we have tried to pay off.

The Ego has to satisfy three task-masters—the Id, Super-ego and Reality—and just as we sometimes can slay any person by working them too hard, so we break down our own Egos every now and again and our whole personality structure goes on the blink.

In this complicated civilized world of today the animal, primitive forces within us, the powerful urges to get what we want—food, comfort, and sexual satisfaction—have to be controlled, modified and disguised and sat on so much that our Egos would seem to have a full-time job.

Pile on top of that Ego's job of riding herd on our equally powerful urges to beat up, ride over and destroy anything or anybody that tries to stop us from doing what we feel like doing, and we can readily understand that Ego has no light assignment in any human being in whom there is a strong, healthy, active drive to *live.*

And finally, pile on top of that, Ego's job of trying to

meet the demands of reality so that others will accept us as "normal" decent citizens.

Let's take a classic line of poetry, "I am the master of my fate." It was penned by a man while lying in a hospital bed. These are brave sentiments but they simply mean that the most he can do is to adjust himself to his sickness.

His Ego may be able to decide what he's going to do with himself, but he isn't going to be able to control and shift *all* the rest of the world around to please his fancy. He (his Ego) can be his own master—only up to a point, as we all can be, when it comes to deciding how we will adjust to Reality (environment outside of us). If we think we don't have to adjust to that reality, we might just as well admit we're escaping to the world of illusion, hallucination, fake and fancy.

When Ego can't measure up to the demands of the third of its three masters, Reality, the whole system of the personality goes off the beam. The Egos of most of us hold their own most of the time. But even some of the everyday problems aren't so easy to face. Sometimes wife's nagging gets to be too much. Sometimes husband's penny-pinching is the last straw. Sometimes mother-in-law's visit lasts too long. Sometimes the boss gets too exacting. Sometimes the bottle is too easy an escape.

Reality—and that's both our friends and our enemies—insists that we take a bath. It insists that we pay our bills, and that we be civil and courteous, sometimes when that is tough.

Besides we have to do that chore of shaving or fixing our hair; we have to wash the dishes; we have to carry out the garbage and we have to clean the hen house. Every day in one way or another Reality is demanding that our Egos perform.

In extreme cases the Ego gives up trying to meet the demands of the world. Then men and women try to avoid

Reality by making up their own little worlds. They desert ours. When they believe that they *are* Napoleon, Julius Caesar, Queen Mary of Scots or Cleopatra, they have left us, too often for good. But they are the rare, rare exceptions.

A more frequent "escape" is one such as that of the man or woman who goes along the street at the close of the working day "really telling the boss off."

"Now you high and mighty so and so, see how much better this shop is run when you listen to me. Look at that pile of money we made just because we did it my way. You're fired. I take over here and now. How do you like that? Etc. Etc." Don't stare at the poor guy or gal. He or she is having fun in a dreamed-up world.

We who regard ourselves as "normal," "average," etc. can see without being upset about it that all of our Egos get a little weary now and then of serving that master, Reality.

In discussing the complicated inter-relations of various parts of human beings, we have to mention again that critic, the Super-Ego, that is sitting on the sidelines to jeer, to point fingers, to condemn every time hard-pressed Ego makes a mistake. Every Ego makes lots of them. If the Super-Ego is a severe one, then life is much tougher. On the other hand, without the Super-Ego we would be in an equally bad state—we would lack ideals and principles. There isn't any way of getting around it—we have to have an internal as well as an external policeman. Let's hope our Egos don't make too many mistakes—and our personal policemen have some bit of understanding.

This brings us to some more of the ways and devices we use; some of the plays and maneuvers we go through as Ego tries to maintain the balance and keep Id, Super-Ego and Reality all satisfied sufficiently to carry us through life without cracking up or destroying ourselves. Those plays, processes and methods we call the Defense

Mechanisms. They serve as defensive measures for the Ego to use to handle the threats against its integrity. There are other mechanisms we use in everyday living to make life a little richer, like sublimation and repression. There are those which are a part of our growth process like identification, introjection and symbolization. All of these have been discussed previously.

MENTAL MECHANISMS

OUR EGO has to take care of us day in and day out by maintaining our balance and enabling us to get along with the outside world. It controls and directs the push and shove of Id while trying to satisfy the critical and tyrannical Super-Ego that can make us miserable if Ego makes what Super-Ego regards as a mistake. When Ego can't maintain that balance, then we are in trouble. Either we clash with the outside world or we suffer within ourselves in one way or another and sometimes break down under the strain. In either case we are likely to develop *Anxiety*—that feeling of distress and concern and tension related to conflict or insecurity.

If we think of Ego as a combination stage door-keeper and director on amateur night we can understand some of his troubles.

Picture a pushing, shoving crowd of energetic kids wanting more than anything else to get out there on that stage and do their stuff. That's all the desires, urges and impulses of Id.

The audience, and it's a hard one to please, is the outside world.

In the wings is an old fellow who is the critic (Super-Ego), and if he doesn't like what Ego lets happen out there, he can make him so sorry he'll want to give up show business.

Ego, poor devil, has to dress some of these kids up and straighten out their act so that they will get by. With others, he knows that if he gives them a nice harmless song or dance routine that everybody likes, they can work off their energy and be satisfied. So will the audience and critic.

In that crowd of impatient youngsters there are bound to be some strapping strong creatures who are straining to get out there and do a strip tease or make obscene gestures that would shock the audience and that critic so badly that it would break up the show and the whole outfit would get slapped into jail or pushed out of town.

If Ego is really on the job and knows his stuff, he can take one of these young bucks or intriguing girls and think up an act that will use that talent so well that the audience will think it's wonderful.

Some of the youngsters will present terrible problems and Ego will have to refuse to let them get out there at all. The weak ones will just hang around and keep on hoping and begging for a chance, but not the strong ones. They'll try anything to get by Ego and out on that stage. They'll disguise themselves as something else, they'll try to crash their way through or sneak around to find a back entrance.

Ego really has his hands full. Sometimes they succeed in getting past him despite all he can do, and then Super-Ego condemns him. If too many get by, the whole audience will object and Ego, his Id gang, and even the old critic will all be put away by society.

These moves, strategies and actions which Ego uses to keep the show going and to allay anxiety are put into motion without our knowing about them. They are what we call the "mechanisms"—they are automatic, dynamic forces.

Ego has to make these moves for three purposes:

1. He has to meet Id's demands somehow; there is too

much drive there to sit on forever; besides the whole personality functions on the energy supplied by the Id.

2. If he wants to stay in business, Ego has to protect himself from two dangers from that audience (outside reality):

A. Ego is afraid to lose his sources of approval or "love." He is always scared of the possibility that people and especially certain persons will dislike him.

B. Ego is afraid that that outside reality will injure or destroy him. He has a healthy fear of real danger and another less obvious fear is fear of hurting himself.

3. Ego tries to protect himself against the danger of loss of approval of the Super-Ego or conscience.

These defense mechanisms operate both in adjustment and in maladjustment. The extent or the degree to which they are used is the real differentiation between health and sickness. It is a matter of quantity and not quality. For instance, one can be a little suspicious (the kind of mechanism we discuss as projection) and yet not necessarily be sick. If, however, an individual's suspicion develops into a chronic belief that the world is persecuting him and has it in for him, then he is ill.

One of the characteristics of these defense mechanisms is that even in health we are rarely aware of using them. However, we can often detect them in others, particularly maladjusted relatives and friends.

Mental health is adjustment, or balance, between conflicting factors both within the personality and between the personality and the environment. In severe personality disorders the psychological equilibrium gets thrown off balance. We need to spend a little extra time at this point to try to explain *how* it is thrown off.

We wish we could make it all very simple, but we can't.

Again part of the trouble is with words. Lay people use certain words to mean a lot of things; whereas the psychiatrists apply these same words with a very limited and specific meaning. Here we refer to two words: *Fear* and *Anxiety*. No matter whose language we use, psychiatrists' or ours, these emotions are important factors in everybody's life. Regardless of what *you* may mean by these words, psychiatrists define *Fear* as that concern and feeling which results from some real external danger—in mild or early stages, it is apprehension. *Anxiety* is the feeling which arises because of threatening danger from internal conflicts.

As a matter of fact we can't always separate them. Sometimes they blend. An exposure to real danger can create Fear, but then when the danger is all past, even the thought of it may cause uneasiness—the reaction of Anxiety.

Sometimes we talk or hear people talk about "fear of high places" or "fear of being in a crowd." This is a still different kind of "fear"—psychiatrists call it a *Phobia*. It represents Anxiety connected with an unconscious conflict and is stimulated only by specific external situations or in connection with specific things.

Of course fear in situations of real danger is healthy. Every combat soldier was afraid—the bravest ones usually admitted it readily. It was helpful to be afraid—up to a limit. It caused the man's muscles to be tense; it turned loose some extra sugar from his liver to provide energy quickly; it contracted his blood vessels and speeded up his heart; it made him more alert. *But*—just up to a limit! Beyond that it might demoralize him. If the fearful experience continued too long it set up a reaction that went on and on, even after the shooting was over for him, so that he still jumped with any sudden—not even loud—noise. He was jittery long after the real danger had passed. Anxiety had succeeded the fear.

Anxiety arises because the balance of control by the Ego is threatened. It is a kind of red flag—it means that something in the trio of Ego, Super-Ego, and Id is out of kilter. Anxiety is the common factor in all kinds of unhealthy mental responses. In some ways it might be compared to pain—it indicates something is wrong.

As far as appearances go, we could say that Fear and Anxiety are identical twins. Whether man, woman or child, if we get in the early clutches of either one, the body goes through the same physical changes. We tremble and are restless, flush hot and cold, our breathing quickens, our pulses beat faster, we sweat, lose our appetite, often suffer nausea or diarrhea and sleep itself is a torture of fitful snatches between nightmares.

But there the twinship ends—right where they both start.

When Ego becomes aware of a train, a car, a flood or even an overdue gas bill coming towards us, Ego calls for action to get rid of it. Our bodies act and we move out of the way of the train, car and flood—if we can. Most of us go into action to make the money to pay the overdue gas bill, but some have been known just to move out of the way of that too.

With any real solution the tenseness that was in us leaves because Ego kept the balance (we say, "we kept our heads or wits") and Id-Super-Ego-Reality were all satisfied. Reality might not be so happy about that unpaid gas bill—but that's not us. The dangers—the threats— that Ego handles in that way are real ones. Fear, arising from threats in the environment, gives rise to uneasiness that the Ego gets rid of by action. This solution prevents any disturbance in its equilibrium with the Id and Super-Ego.

When our equilibrium is threatened by the disturbance that we call Anxiety, what happens then? The tenseness associated with Anxiety comes from within ourselves, and

is the result of our Ego being made uncomfortable because of the demands made upon it by Id and Super-Ego.
Anxiety arises without regard to a threat in the current
environment.

The unconscious part of the Ego becomes aware of the
pressure of an impulse threatening from the Id. One of
those buried (repressed) conflicts is about to burst forth.
The Ego feels its control is threatened. That *feeling* is
Anxiety. Ego has to act fast—it has to protect itself—it
must try to maintain its control. And here is where it
brings in its bag of tricks—automatic unconscious defense devices to channel off that impulse.

We should not give the impression that the Ego and
its defense mechanisms are like a card player with a hand
of cards. It doesn't sit on the sideline objectively and
pick out a particular mechanism to play in a specific situation. The Ego uses the patterns of reaction which developed in childhood. As certain ones proved most effective in meeting our needs they were used to the exclu-
sion of others. Each of us has a battery of tested methods
of getting gratification; specific (for us) methods of defending ourselves. Throughout life each particular individual continues to use, in general, those reactions
which he has found most expedient for himself. Thus
some of us use certain defense mechanisms and not others.
The choice of the mechanisms that one uses depends then
first and chiefly on childhood experiences. Secondarily,
the choice is determined by the particular situation or
problem against which the Ego needs to defend itself.

Several of the defense mechanisms are used rather extensively by most of us most every day. By their use we
are able to remain effective and more or less satisfied
with life. In other words, we stay relatively healthy—
at least within normal limits—by finding channels for
impulses to express themselves which are satisfactory to
our conscious selves and to our environment.

Those defense mechanisms whose expressions are relatively healthy are technically called, *Compensation, Rationalization, Idealization, Reaction Formation* and *Displacement.* Any of them can be used to the extreme, that is to such excessive degrees that they cause too much disturbance in the environment and thus cheat us out of our effectiveness or our satisfaction in life. But most of the time they protect the Ego from any sense of anxiety by providing an apparent resolution of internal conflicts.

On the other hand, there are at least three of our defence mechanisms—*Projection, Undoing* and *Conversion*—which almost always represent psycho-pathology, that is, symptoms. They are more transparent in their irrationality. Their more pronounced expressions are almost always recognizable symptoms of maladjustment. In their larval stages, many people keep on with their jobs or their relationships without too much discomfort to themselves or to others. Even so their use is always evidence of an unhealthy state. They may become the conspicuous features of severe maladjustment.

The use of the defense mechanism is always an attempted compromise of conflicting forces. The Ego wants to take one course and the Id another. The behavior resulting from the use of the mechanism, whether as suspicion or obsessions or a physical symptom, represents a compromise which gives some degree of satisfaction to both the Ego and the Id.

We have explained that the defense mechanisms are the ways that the Ego uses to protect itself against anxiety. When the impulse that is threatening to escape from the Id (which is the reason for the Ego's anxiety) is permitted release through one of these mechanisms, the anxiety or acute feeling of tenseness or uneasiness is to some extent relieved. The manifestation of the mechanism, that is its expression, is a kind of "solution" of the conflict between the Id and the Ego.

For instance, a soldier in combat develops great fear because of the imminent danger to which he is exposed. But he knows it is unmilitary to escape or hide and so he represses and denies such impulses, though a strong feeling of anxiety remains. In many cases the fear stirs up unconscious conflicts and so causes anxiety. With one particular type of conflict, he may suddenly develop a paralysis of the arm without being hit by a shell. Following the development of such "hysterical" paralysis, his anxiety diminishes.

Whereas his Ego would not tolerate his desertion from duty because of his fear when that was disguised as a disability to his shooting arm, he could save face with Ego and satisfy Id. The conflict arising in the Id in the presence of a specific reality demand, was temporarily, at least, solved. All this, remember, went on below and entirely outside his conscious thinking.

Many times the solution, that is, the permitted expression of the conflict (or of the repressed urge) through the mechanism, is not sufficient to relieve the anxiety. In such cases the Ego can elaborate and intensify its use of the defense mechanism: for instance, mild suspiciousness turns into fixed ideas of persecution. In other cases, even though the defense mechanism is used extensively, the person still may feel anxious and tense and uneasy. Such usage of defense mechanisms is definite mental illness.

The defense mechanisms, either because of the particular one used or the intensity of their use, may be accompanied with physical or mental discomfort. Thus, stomach disorder, resulting from emotional turmoil, may have just as much real physical discomfort as an inflammation of the lining of the stomach. A person with a phobia can only be comfortable if there isn't any threat in the immediate environment. A person, afraid of high places, is comfortable *only* on the ground. While these mechanisms keep us healthy in some instances, they give us pain in others.

Let us discuss first those defense mechanisms whose common expressions are accepted as being within the range of normal behavior. All of them have a common end—they allow our Egos to keep the "show going" without Id, Super-Ego or the world outside becoming too upset. The personality uses them without our knowledge to help us keep our balance. Our peace of mind is maintained by means of these mechanisms, which are called compensation, rationalization, idealization, reaction formation and displacement.

COMPENSATION

Compensation is a mechanism that the Ego uses to defend itself against anxiety caused by a feeling of insecurity, by making extra effort in an area of real or fancied weakness. Some men and women of great achievement are good examples of this dynamism in operation:

Milton in his blindness wrote magnificent literature, and Beethoven composed his great symphonies while growing more and more deaf. We see evidence of Compensation all around us where physical or mental, real or imagined handicaps have led people to strive to make up for those deficiencies.

Who doesn't know the little man or woman who, to put it bluntly, makes a "big noise" to compensate for his or her "inferiority." Some people become objectionable to us in the way that they constantly try to create the impression that they are important, intelligent or very profound thinkers. These have their counterparts in the big individuals who over-react to their size. Well-balanced little ones and well-balanced big ones don't disturb us;

in fact they often contribute to our common good through their Compensations.

Persons with bad teeth, disfigured faces, deformed limbs all develop methods of compensating for these which are entirely unrecognized by themselves, though often apparent to others. Then there are still other people who are so much too honest, too hardworking, or too liberal that they make even their friends wonder why they go to such extremes.

There is one form of Compensation that we frequently don't recognize as such in ourselves as much as in others, and that is *Substitution*.

The father and mother who don't give their child the love, consideration and attention that unconsciously they feel they should, are likely to substitute a big fuzzy teddy bear or some such gift to compensate for that neglect. A little later on it's cash. Many of us know fathers who are so wound up in their own affairs that about their only contact with their son or daughter is the giving of too-liberal allowances.

Sometimes the guilty parties recognize what they are doing, but for every one who does, there are scores who do not.

That is what happened when Mr. Jones, without realizing why, decided he *ought* to take home a box of candy on the day he took a deep look into the eyes of that new secretary. And why Mrs. Jones thought she ought to bake her husband's favorite cake after she read a new mystery instead of mending his shirts. They are running one of the personality's trick plays of dressing up the unapproved behavior in a Compensation.

Lest we convey an incomplete idea, all of us need and are helped by Compensations of some types. They make us strive harder like the less intelligent student who works very hard for his excellent grades. Becoming an expert in one field because of inabilities in another may provide confidence otherwise absent. Efforts toward Compensation may lead to the development of latent abilities just as blindness increases the sensitivity of touch.

RATIONALIZATION

With this trick, the Ego has an easy way to defend itself against anxiety.

Who of us hasn't worked the *conscious* equivalent of this dynamism time and time again? *Rationalization* is the device which we use to defend certain feelings, ideas or behavior by explaining very convincingly and apparently logically that they are the result of something other than the demands of our irrational Ids. When we justify our actions to others by consciously cooking up excuses, that is something else. When we *sincerely believe* that "fate," "luck," "bad breaks," etc. are responsible for all our misfortunes, we are fooling ourselves by Rationalizing.

When we don't want to do something, it is amazing how many "logical" reasons we can think up that keep us from doing it. But if it is something we would really enjoy doing, we think only about the justifications for it. The wonderful part of it is that we have no doubt about the wisdom or correctness or honesty of our thinking when we rationalize.

One of the best demonstrations of Rationalization to watch in process is a twelve-year-old faced with the assignment of mowing the lawn and the desire to play ball with the gang on Saturday.

Listen to his arguments for the ball game and against lawn mowing, and then stand by for the explosion when you accuse him of Rationalization. He honestly believes in what he's saying. So do we all under comparable circumstances.

We don't very frequently pin ourselves down to explaining our ideas or our behavior, but when we do try it, we find it difficult to be honest about why: We like blue or pink; prefer blondes—or brunettes; fall in love with our wife or husband; think dishwashing is "woman's work;" know the kids would just as soon have a sandwich today as a hot-cooked meal; etc., etc. We give a lot of answers, but are they the real ones?

Very often the strings of little white lies we tell ourselves, and believe, are devices that are helpful to our Egos, but they sometimes can get out of hand. When we are convinced that we never make a mistake and everything that goes wrong for us is the doing of somebody else or something else, then we are rationalizing dangerously and our balance is badly upset. The individual who sincerely *believes* that the best way to escape his troubles or his sorrow is to guzzle alcohol, is rationalizing on all eight cylinders.

IDEALIZATION

A specific modification of rationalization is the defense mechanism that is called *Idealization*. In its mild form it amuses us, but pushed to extremes it can become objectionable.

The young lover who really believes the adored one is "the most beautiful (handsome), sweetest, most wonderful human being who ever trod the earth," is working Idealization for all that it is worth, and up to a point we don't object.

But the person who just as firmly thinks that he or she, himself or herself, is flawless, we seldom, if ever, find attractive.

We are all prone to overlook a lot of faults in ourselves that we spot very quickly in others. When we miss detecting even our big and bad ones, then it is time to try to check this self-idealization that is running away with us.

Idealization, when applied to oneself, is a kind of narcissism. It can—and fortunately does—exist in a healthy form in most of us. There are perhaps a few totally selfless people, totally unselfish. But for most of us, *we* are the most important person to us. We can never be quite objective about ourselves; we can't stand by and see ourselves pass in review. We're never able "to see oursel's as others see us." But most of us do want to look well, to impress others favorably, to be well thought of by our friends and associates. To do this means we have to have some self-confidence, self-assurance, and a reasonable faith in our intelligence. This all sums up to a necessary—and healthy—Idealization of ourselves.

REACTION FORMATION

Reversal is another name sometimes used for the method or mechanism that is called *Reaction Formation.*

Sometimes the unconscious has such a strong urge to express itself in one direction that the only way the conscious can control it (and the Ego thereby avoid anxiety) is to do the opposite. In order for the personality to keep from falling forward, it has to lean a long ways backward. Consequently, where we have a deep, powerful, unconscious conflict, we may do the opposite of the original desire. We develop a "reaction" against the urge.

Some of our slips of speech give us away on this point, especially when we are trying very hard to be courteous to somebody we thoroughly dislike. One of the most embarrassing experiences many of us have is that of saying what our unconscious feels when we are trying to be polite. On parting with somebody we don't like at all, it's an easy slip to say, "Don't come and see us," instead of the "Do come and see us," that we thought we intended.

As we have seen, many of the worth-while character

traits we have as adults had their origin back in our earliest childhood when we were having our toilet training. We come into the world with the opposite of desires to be clean, neat, orderly and punctual. As a denial of the original tabooed interests in self-pleasure, the Ego's defense in some people is to do the opposite with a vengeance.

Some of the commonest acts in the daily lives of many of us are *compulsive defenses.* By this we refer to unexplained self-imposed requirements of behavior. Some of us drive ourselves at our work. Sometimes compulsiveness takes the form of making us do things in a particular way. Sometimes it has to do with orderliness, with punctuality, with cleanliness. Sometimes it makes some of us concern ourselves with details, diagrams and charts, organization and tabulation. All of these are illustrations of a comfortable method of expression that the Ego uses and thus prevents the development of anxiety.

In many ways these types of expressions are helpful. They can be very valuable. Also they can cause us distress at times: Perhaps we can't sit still or are uncomfortable without realizing why when we see a picture or the window shades hanging askew or a desk in disorder. We know we are downright uncomfortable when we go into a friend's house and find everything in disorder. We can hardly resist commenting on the fact that the dishes haven't been washed for several meals. We want to tell Jim Smith to use better manners when we see him carelessly knock his cigarette ashes on the rug wherever he happens to be. We just can't stand what, by our code of living, is messiness.

When we lean over backwards to be so orderly that we flare up if the maid displaces the inkwell an inch; when we suffer if the piano is dusty; when we must continually run around emptying the ash trays, the chances are that our behavior is a Reaction Formation.

Then we all know some folks whose urge may still be "normal" but it goes a lot further: their home is so clean and orderly that we wonder if anyone really "lives" in it; we feel uncomfortable just sitting in it. There are those wives whose only mission in life is a continuous chase after dirt, and the vigor and intensity of their pursuit is almost symptomatic. There are those men of whom one gets the impression that a tiny spot on their clothing is far more painful to them than a blot on their reputation. One can be very sure that these types of behavior are Reaction Formations.

It can be considered as a Reversal of strong unconscious desires to be as carefree and sloppy as a hobo living on the city dumps. We rarely realize that our unconscious desires of the moment are often contrary to our conscious ones, all because of our training and the forming of our attitudes which took place so long ago. However, these may show up when the Ego loses control of the situation, as in a psychosis, delirium or drunkenness. Then the painfully polite person often becomes rude and rambunctious; the overly neat and precise become messy and careless.

DISPLACEMENT

Displacement is a mechanism by which the emotional value attached to one idea or person is transferred to another idea or person. Often therefore the emotional attitude expressed toward an object is either out of proportion to it, or even unrelated to it. This again is a defense mechanism for Ego.

When we displace our positive feelings of love, it is a "good" mechanism; when we displace some of our negative ones of hate to other people, it is a "bad" mechanism.

The wife who beats up the dishpan or barks at her child because her husband won't take her to a dance, is trying to *displace* her feelings.

Let that same husband come home, volunteer to take his wife to the dance and throw in a corsage to boot, and she probably will give the cat an extra bowl of milk and be nice and friendly even to a bill collector the next day. This mechanism is in operation whenever the feeling we have toward someone or something is in part or wholly expressed to another. It is present whenever we unknowingly misplace blame or credit for our thoughts or actions.

How often when in school and college we take it out on the friend or roommate when we have had a tough day! Ask the wife or husband of anyone who works in a department store if they were ever on the receiving end of a Displacement. When the "customer is always right," even if the customer is actually a crabby, unreasonable, arrogant so and so, the poor clerk who can never talk back or cut loose with what he or she would like to say, just has to blow off that steam somewhere. More often than not it's the folks at home who are the victims.

It's a pretty good rule for comfortable living to try to catch ourselves whenever we are blaming someone else with great emotion, to see if we aren't Displacing.

If something normally trivial in its importance has us ready to pop a blood vessel, we are very probably transferring to it our feelings about something else that really hasn't any connection with what we are mad about. When we are worried and scared about something, we are frequently cross and short-tempered with those nearest us at the time. They have the misfortune to be convenient targets for the feelings that we are cutting loose.

We would probably get little thanks from a man who is angry because he has just lost his wad in a poker game if we told him to go home and mow his lawn or chop down a tree. But he might easily be doing his wife and children a big favor if he really did it.

We are all too familiar with the dyspeptics who are chronically grouchy and cranky. They don't stop at being sore at people; they get mad at everything from insects to circus parades.

Mothers and teachers who have so much contact with children while they are forming their life patterns would do well to try to evaluate their own emotional demonstrations to see that they don't make the wrong Displacements. In the case of the teacher, the demands *we* make on them and the salaries we pay them in return would almost justify their beating up *our* children every morning right after roll call. It might be almost a warranted Displacement!

And now for those defenses of the Ego against Anxiety which more often represent a poorer adjustment and symptom expression.

PROJECTION

This is a mechanism that we wouldn't brag about if we knew we were using it.

Projection is one of these trick plays by which we dump our own mean wishes and our faults onto somebody else. The Ego uses this defense to disown the unacceptable thoughts shoved at it by the Id, and by so doing always makes the person doing the projecting the object of special consideration or lack of consideration, favor or disfavor. In all cases he tries to become the recipient of attention.

Chronic hard-luck artists are forever doing it. How often we have listened to the person who blames all of his or her troubles on the boss, the wife or husband, acquaintances, children, the cat, the dog, the weather, anything or anybody in the whole wide world except him or her self.

A bit stronger use of this device is unwarranted suspicion—of wife, of husband, of the boss, of most anyone. In such cases the person thinks he is always the center of some special attention. In most instances where this symptom occurs, the attention is regarded as malicious, hostile, destructive. Much less frequently the special "imaginary" consideration is manifested in overevaluation of the self, with special powers, capacity or ability, and certain "events" or "remarks" or "signs" are always cited as proof by the person of his claims.

There aren't any really "healthy" examples of Projection, though some of us use it in such mild forms our friends let us get away with it.

The bridge player who really believes it's always his partner's mistake is a fairly common example that we tolerate but don't particularly like.

One of the most universal forms of Projection is the business of finding a scapegoat. As individuals or nations, we choose certain other individuals or groups of people or races—or even nations—onto which we project our own fears and troubles. It is as if we each have a devil within us which we refuse to acknowledge or admit, and find an outlet by accusing someone else—or a group— of being that devil. *Prejudice* is a rationalized Projection which, like all Projection, is a method of defending the Ego against Anxiety. It's an easy (and unforgivable) way to get rid of some of our own faults or fears.

In the supercharged political atmosphere of today, we might hasten to add that this goes for Yugoslavians and Russians, as well as for Britishers and Americans and, in passing, probably for Terra del Fuegians too.

Projection is often very much in evidence in some of the persons who are so extremely maladjusted that they have to be taken to the hospital for their own good. They are the ones who "know" that certain individuals and sometimes practically the whole world is in on a plot to do them wrong. The fear of their own unconscious wishes demands that they find someone to blame other than themselves. They are said to have *paranoid delusions*

—meaning that they have unfounded but very fixed ideas of persecution.

UNDOING

The second type of defense mechanism that the Ego uses commonly as a substitute expression for Anxiety is known as *Undoing*. Just as in the case of the other mechanisms, there are harmless examples in the "normal" person of Undoing that many of our Egos use to keep us happy. These are mostly tied up in our superstitions. They are unconscious attempts to undo or blot out through some symbolic act an experience or impression that is painful to the Ego.

For the purpose of illustration, some common conscious acts are related to this mechanism. Many persons have a habit of "knocking on wood" or "touching wood." If we have bragged about something or wished for something so much that we fear we might be punished for doing so, that uncomfortable feeling is removed for many of us by performing this ceremony of touching wood.

Crossing our fingers for luck, avoiding walking under a ladder, turning around three times if a black cat crosses our path, saying "bread and butter" if someone or something separates us temporarily from our friend, and many other little devices illustrate how we gain a feeling of correcting or rectifying or Undoing a particular act or situation. But these are conscious and probably are related to well-recognized feelings of omnipotence in baby hood.

There are certain types of symbolic rituals that become desperately necessary to us sometimes. They ease our consciences; some give us hope and faith; some bribe our tyrannical Super-Egos so as to enable us to believe in ourselves and the world.

This defense, however, can be carried to an extreme which makes life extremely difficult. Simple life activities such as washing one's hands may become compulsory and unreasonable and frequently repeated ceremonials or rituals for the person who can't stand the anxiety if he doesn't perform them. In these instances the expressions of the mechanism are serious symptoms of maladjustment and illness because they prevent "normal" living.

CONVERSION

This mechanism is the method the Ego uses to defend itself against anxiety by directing the expression of repressed wishes into physical symptoms. The mental conflict thereby directly influences the comfort and function of the body. It was the mechanism that was used so often during the war by G.I. and General alike, when the going was rugged, expressed in the immortal phrase, "Oh! My aching back."

Sometimes the impulse which causes the emotional conflict is "converted" into a mistaken idea about the environment like a fear of harm from dirt, or some disease. Much more often, however, the *Conversion* takes place right within our bodies and is expressed in physical symptoms. Before discussing Conversion in detail, we might advisedly take a little longer look at this relationship between the mind (the emotions) and the physical part of us.

PSYCHE VERSUS SOMA

Mankind has known for a long time that the state of the *Psyche* (mind-emotions) has something to do with the state of the *Soma* (body). The old Greek ideal of a healthy mind in a sound body acknowledged that the two were closely related. Yet today many people have a hard time admitting even to themselves that this is so.

In fact their faces will turn lobster red with rage or ash gray with cold fury when we tell them that their thoughts and emotions affect their bodies and (very often) are responsible for many of their aches and pains. It is difficult to understand how, in such a state, they can look into a mirror or count their own pulse beats and still deny any connection between what they *feel* and how their body is *behaving*.

The stresses and strains that were laid upon all our Egos during the war gave many of us new and greater appreciation of the close interrelation between our thoughts and feelings and the functioning of our physical selves.

Many mothers and wives found that they just had to find ways to "work off" or "blow off" the tension caused by the worry over the comfort and safety of sons and husbands. Millions of those sons and husbands in the armed forces, on the merchant ships and in other war activity where the pressure was great, discovered many things about their emotions and the effect of these on their bodies they had never known before.

One of the commonest things these men learned was that when life was awfully tough over a long period they were prone to develop physical symptoms—their hearts or their lungs, their eyes or their stomachs, or some other part of them didn't work right. They couldn't control or avoid the symptoms any more than the guy trying to make a speech can keep his knees from knocking or his hands from sweating.

In that latter case, just as in every pronounced emotional reaction—fear, love, hate, excitement, anger—there are some automatic responses by various organs of the body. The wobbling knees and the sweating hands are just as truly a part of the transient emotional reaction as is the fear that the speaker feels.

In contrast to the physical aspects of the emotional

response to a temporary situation are those physical symptoms caused by deep-seated psychological conflicts. In the former there is ordinarily no physical pain and often minimal discomfort. One doesn't go to the physician about them. In the latter—the Conversion symptoms—there is almost always physical pain or incapacity and sooner or later one may be forced to seek medical help for their relief.

In the Conversion mechanism the Ego channels the tabooed impulse arising from the deeper layers of unconsciousness into some type of physical symptom. The impulse was converted (disguised) into a physical reaction, hence the term Conversion symptom.

Initially, psychiatrists used this term to apply only to those cases in which the emotion arising from an unrecognized conflict became pinned down in some section of the body that was under voluntary control. Such symptoms could be seen and demonstrated: an "hysterical" paralysis of the arm, loss of sensitivity of the skin (anesthesia) or a loss of the voice. They were identified as "hysterical" * when no physical basis for the symptoms could be found. Some physicians still limit the use of *Conversion Reaction* to these few conditions. Many psychiatrists, however, now consider that all disorders of function of any organ in the body that are related to an unconscious psychic conflict are Conversion symptoms. Thus, they may be manifested by palpitations of the heart, a nervous stomach, intestinal cramps, as well as the functional paralysis or loss of the voice.

Conversion symptoms are just as real as a fever. Few things will irritate the sufferer more than to tell him to

* For years the scientific diagnosis has been "conversion hysteria." The term "hysteria" comes from the Greek word, hystera, meaning uterus. Originally it was believed that this disorder occurred only in women and was caused by the uterus breaking loose from its moorings and wandering over the body, exerting pressure on nerves and organs.

"forget it" or that the complaint is "all in his mind." The pain itself is as real as that from a broken leg. Our physical troubles which start in our "minds" arise from the unconscious and therefore the possessor doesn't know either its cause or its true meaning. Such Conversions of psychological conflicts are common—very common. The army and navy doctors found, as physicians do every day, that a lot of the pains and ills of human beings have no organic basis—that is, no germs or ten-ton trucks came in from the outside to cause internal injury. The conflicts *within* the patient's own personality gave rise to the physical discomfort.

Those physical expressions that are component parts of a transient emotional response ordinarily pass when the original stimulus for the emotional reaction is gone. The exception to this is when that stimulus is constant for long periods. The best example of such a case was the experience of the soldier in combat, where for days on end he was threatened with death every minute. It is not surprising that this prolonged state of fear did things to him—both psychologically and physically. His "normal" reaction to fear often kept on long after the shooting. It became pathological, and the physiological and physical components of his reaction became Conversion Reactions.

Some Conversion symptoms that persist for long periods bring about physical changes. A functional paralysis will result in a wasting of the muscles. A "nervous stomach" in which there is a prolonged disturbance of secretion and muscle spasm may eventually result in a stomach ulcer. Other types of physical changes can and do take place as a result of prolonged unconscious emotional conflict.

Up to this point, we have been discussing chiefly the Psyche and Soma relationships as they are expressed in the mental mechanism of Conversion. These are very important because they make up a high percentage of the illnesses seen in about half the patients of a general practice. In fact, the medical profession has become very much aware of the connection between our Psyches and our Somas, our emotions and our physical states. Recently they have coined the term *psycho-somatic medicine* to refer to a point of view which regards all illness—even health —as having a psychological as well as physical aspect both in its causes and manifestations.

It isn't even very important for us to try to define here the differences between the physical expressions of a passing emotional reaction and true Conversion symptoms. It *is* important for us to emphasize the close, the inseparable relationship between the Psyche and the Soma. The manifestations that we meet with in our friends, associates and enemies (and ourselves) are lodged most commonly in four different areas of the Soma or Body. "Feeling the way we do" can cause a disturbance in the cardiovascular system (heart and blood vessels) or in the gastro-intestinal system (the digestive tract from "stem to stern"), or in the muscles and joints or the genito-urinary system that takes care of both propagating the race and urinating.

Let's start with the heart which our Valentine custom implies is the most vital part of us. The importance of this particular organ is so emphasized all our lives, that practically any of us would rather listen to a doctor telling us that our kidneys were shot to ribbons than to have him say that our heart skipped beats now and then. If our hearts start pounding, speeding up, or slowing way down without obvious provocation, we are likely to be conscious of it, and wonder what it means and why. Some of us are apt to go galloping off to the nearest doctor. Most soldiers in combat became aware that their hearts were doing something out of the ordinary. Medical books used to list a condition, "Soldier's heart," seen in many soldiers in whom there are no organic changes in the heart. With slight physical effort it just beats too fast. Civilian doctors identify this as "effort syndrome," where it occurs in plain-clothes men, but it's still the same kind of pounding, no matter who has it or what it is called.

If we really believe that how we feel or what we are thinking doesn't have anything to do with our bodies, our hearts shouldn't beat any faster or slower at a strawberry festival than in a foxhole. It does though; and the number of physically healthy men and women in civilian life who are knocked out of commission every year by the reaction of their hearts to their attitudes and methods of living is far too high.

Not only our hearts but the whole set of blood vessels, including the little coronary artery on the surface of the heart, may become involved in our emotions. It should not be surprising that sometimes violent fits of temper, or very great disappointments, or for that matter many other kinds of emotion are associated with coronary disease. Nor should it surprise us to find that some people who live at high tension year in and year out show varying degrees of high blood pressure. We can't be tense or react violently day after day to something we don't like without its doing things to us. Overworked prejudices can burst blood vessels just as effectively as bullets or too much atmospheric pressure if we give them enough time and exercise.

Our gastro-intestinal tracts (we usually speak of them as our digestive systems) are seriously affected by our emotions in a lot of different ways. Maybe that's because they are partly under our voluntary control (we can eat or not, as we choose, and go to the toilet or not when we choose). Whatever the cause, this portion of our bodies seems to be affected by our emotions more than any other.

Next to the skin, the gastro-intestinal system has more contact with the outside world than any other part of us. It has to adjust and accommodate to more direct demands made on it, takes more insults and punishment, and has more varied opportunities for gratification than any other set of organs. We starve it, stuff it, diet and doctor it till it's often a wonder it works at all.

Just let our emotions disturb us and the innocent bystander who gets involved practically every time is the gastrointestinal system—with loss of appetite, nausea, indigestion, constipation, etc., etc. A little boy's stomach is likely to be badly "upset" when his dog dies, just as his father's is when the pressure is too heavy on him down at the office.

In addition to reflecting our emotional conflicts, this system rather clearly illustrates many other psychosomatic relationships in health, as well as minor and transient emotional flurries. Our infantile experiences with this system were in large measure responsible for our patterns of expression of all attitudes related to taking in or receiving, holding onto, retaining or giving up and finally eliminating or giving.

We often associate food and love. *Tea for Two,* a Fourth of July clambake or barbecue, or two soldiers under fire, splitting a C-ration are all demonstrations of the enhancement of our social relationships by eating. There is good evidence to relate overeating in some cases with unconscious insecurity or need for love. We use this system also symbolically to reject—a child may vomit if he doesn't want to do something. Diarrhea—as rejection—may be related to fear. Constipation may often be related to prolonged tension.

Personality is often expressed so revealingly through this system, by eating habits, food choices and quantity, as well as in toilet habits. All of us know people who go on year in and year out with a boring picayunish faddism about their eating which is so often a reflection of a basic uncertainty and insecurity. Gourmets have a specific personality twist which makes fine and rare foods a compensatory satisfaction. Methods of eating and table manners may be disturbing revelations of personality traits. For some persons toilet habits become overevaluated, so much so that in their private life, a bowel movement is the most important—at least the most essential—event of the day. Fear of constipation becomes a continuous bugaboo and a nightly laxative becomes routine.

Also the recognition of a relationship between Soma and Psyche is illustrated by our colloquial vocabulary. When we use terms such as "sink your teeth into a job," "bite off more than we can chew," "have guts," or "have had a belly full" we are unconsciously linking actions of this system with our emotional attitudes toward life.

Disorders in function of many other sets of bodily organs occurred frequently in the soldier and the sailor just as they do in our daily civilian life. The complaints of low back pains, sore and aching muscles, and creaking joints can be heard in any boarding house just as well as in any barracks.

Impotence in men and frigidity in women, those two wreckers of romance and satisfactory marriage, are so closely bound into our emotions of love and hate, and our fears and worries that the connection cannot be denied with real conviction by any intelligent person in spite of the absence of laboratory proof.

Our belief that "Mind over Matter" or "Matter over Mind" may be important to us as individuals in "getting the most out of life." But a realization that our Psyches and our Somas are inseparably fused through that life is important in the understanding of why we feel the way we do.

SUMMARY OF THE MECHANISMS

Having paraded these mechanisms, the machinery of our psychological life, it might be well to tie them together a little bit along with one or two other points about ourselves.

As we've tried to illustrate, some of these mechanisms have as their chief function the business of keeping us well. The presence of others of them always indicates that we are sick. Most of them can function either way: all of them are automatic and that means that they function with no conscious intent or effort or knowledge on our part.

At times we all experience anxieties or fears. Many of us are subject to physical symptoms when we become emotionally upset. Almost every one of us has some eccentricities or mannerisms or methods of action or ideas that mark him as "abnormal." There is probably no one who doesn't have some difficulties or deviations from the "normal" in his sex life.

The war focused so much attention on the personality, and particularly on personality difficulties, that there was one great lesson which a lot of people seemed to learn for the first time. Many of the rest of us were equally impressed with it. That lesson was that when we are taken out of a little world where we've been relatively protected, and are thrown into a bigger and rougher world, our Egos have to do a lot of readjusting to keep us well enough to get along.

The new worlds of army or navy life or life without a husband or father or son with all their demands and pressures were more than thousands of Egos were strong enough to take. The toughest, healthiest and strongest Ego in the world can stand only so much.

Adjusting to the demands of military service in war time was anything but easy, and Selective Service Boards refused to accept 1,850,000 men in this country because they were regarded as poor psychiatric risks. That was 38% of all the citizens who were of draft age who were rejected for all reasons.

Hundreds of thousands of these men had gotten along

well and successfully in the environment they had accepted and adjusted to as their own. But from experience, it had been found that many of these could not adjust sufficiently to military life to become good soldiers.

More than half a million men, 49% of all discharges from the army for mental or physical defects, were discharged because of their inability to make the adjustments demanded of them.

Some failed after only a few weeks in training camp. Others fought like tigers through battle after battle until the continuing strain was too great even for their previously strong and well-adjusted personalities.

None of those men were any "crazier" or more "insane" than you or I.

Men in war "falter" and lose their usefulness as soldiers in the same ways and for the same kinds of reasons that men become incapacitated as participating members of society.

The pounding of German 88 guns and the diving Japanese Kamikazi planes are totally different stresses from living with a wife and three kids in the attic of an in-law's house or not being able to find a job. But the effect on the personality is very much the same.

Ego does the best it can, but sooner or later, in this complex civilization it may be overcome by troubles that result in hurt and worry. These hurts and these worries are symptoms. They are symptoms of ill health just like fever or swelling. The fact that they aren't always recognized as such doesn't change one whit the fact that they are evidences of ill health.

Symptoms of emotional conflict can become so severe that they incapacitate a personality for living normally. In such a case, the personality is emotionally ill, a mental sickness falling most often into either of two large groups known as *Psychoses* and *Neuroses*.

When one develops a Psychosis, he becomes irrational in varying degrees. In fact, the delirium with a fever is a kind of Psychosis. A Psychosis in popular terms is referred to (incorrectly) as "insanity." (Insane, correctly used, is a legal concept and not medical.) In a Psychosis, the individual has fixed mistaken ideas unamenable to reason (delusions). In some instances the patient may persistently and consistently misinterpret the things he sees and hears (illusions). In a very few cases, he may even hear, see, feel, taste or smell things that are not there (hallucinations).

The Psychoses have absorbed the major part of psychiatric effort to date. Some 600,000 persons now in our state hospitals and probably many thousands more in other hospitals, at home or in "homes" are suffering from Psychoses. They represent a different type of mental illness from the Neuroses, not in the nature of the psychological processes in a qualitative way but markedly in a quantitative way. The individual with a Neurosis can and does keep oriented to the things and world about him, whereas the individual with a Psychosis has to deny or distort or misconstrue some one or more aspects of his environment in varying degrees.

It is believed that a Psychosis results in individuals whose personality development has presented greater deflections from the ideal, where the Ego was more severely incapacitated in its function of controlling the Id's demands in relation to external reality. Sometimes the Ego has been weakened because of physical damage to some part of the body, particularly the brain—infection, injury, and other causes. Then there is no doubt that the external stress, its type and duration, also has much to do in bringing about a partial disintegration of the personality that results in a Psychosis.

The principle of treatment is just the same in both the Neuroses and Psychoses in that the patient must be helped to face his problem and find a solution rather than attempting to escape from it.

Even though Psychoses are in some ways more severe illnesses than Neuroses, the outlook for recovery is good when treatment is early. This was demonstrated in the army, when during 1945 we were able to send 7 out of 10 soldiers who had had psychotic reactions, to their homes. Only 3 out of 10 had to go to state or veteran's hospitals for further care or treatment. Even with inadequate staffs and facilities, our state hospitals return forty percent of new admissions each year to their homes, sufficiently readjusted to carry on their previous activities.

The Neuroses are far more frequent than Psychoses. At times we *all* have neurotic symptoms. When our Id impulses are not sublimated and our repressions gain expression, they appear as unhealthy displacements, compensations, conversions, and in many other forms. These are *neurotic symptoms*. Some of us live with them day in and day out and just keep on with our regular activities. In fact, neurotic personalities have contributed beyond measure to our culture and science. Our symptoms may make us uncomfortable and handicap us but usually don't stop us.

Sometimes, however, they get pretty intense. Sometimes they multiply until they knock us out and actually incapacitate us. It's at that point that if we go to any doctor who is at home in the realm of psychiatry, we are given a diagnosis of *neurosis* or *psychoneurosis*. (The words are used interchangeably and mean the same thing.) This means we are "nervous" or emotionally upset. The severity varies widely but the chances for relief and recovery are excellent if one gets help early. Approximately sixty percent of our soldiers who broke down in combat *went back* to more combat. Thirty percent more could go back to various forms of non-combat duty. There are, of course, persons who remain sick for years; there are life-long neurotic invalids. Some cases require long-term help with psychoanalytic treatment. But the great majority can, if treated early, entirely readjust.

Many persons have the idea that individuals don't get over nervousness or mental illness. Goodness knows we all get upset often enough to realize that in most instances we do come out of it quite all right. One special hope that we have in writing this book is that we may debunk at least some of the fears and the mystery about mental ill health, particularly the silly bugaboo that people don't get well or they are, after a mental illness, in some way a permanent liability to themselves and society.

CHAPTER VIII

IF YOU GO TO THE
PSYCHIATRIST

SOONER OR later most of us have to go to the doctor, or he has to come see us. This happens in ordinary physical illnesses frequently enough so that we usually know about what to expect. We know that the chances are that he'll look down our throats and thump our chests, listen to our hearts and maybe stick our fingers with a needle to get a drop or two of blood. Depending upon what our particular illness is, we have a pretty fair notion as to what kind of treatment we'll receive—perhaps some medicine, some changes in our diet, some specific instructions as to how much physical activity we may undertake, possibly an operation advised.

Most of us are pretty hazy about what would happen if we went to a psychiatrist. Few know what to expect in the way of his various treatment procedures. Consulting him, however, is essentially no different from going to any other physician, except that the psychiatrist, just as any other specialist, has his particular methods for examining and treating.

The extent or nature of the problem determines the extensiveness of the examination. With a complex problem, the chances are that the psychiatrist will give an elaborate and extensive examination.

Of major importance is a life history which is obtained by asking many questions of you or your relatives. The questions may seem to have little or nothing to do with the immediate problem at hand. If the psychiatrist is fortunate enough to have a psychiatric social worker, the chances are he'll have her question the patient in great detail regarding certain areas of his life experience. The clinical psychologist will give a series of personality tests, the results of which will indicate an amazing number of facts. The psychiatrist will make use of these but he may not attempt to explain to you the results of specific tests.

Certainly you will have a physical examination including your heart, lungs, abdomen—just as when you go to your regular physician. In addition, you will surely have a neurological examination—a special going-over of your nervous system. This includes your vision, hearing, smell and the functions of all the other nerves of your head and face (they are called the cranial nerves); the motor (muscle actions) and sensory systems; the reflexes, which we discussed in the first chapter, coordination, equilibrium, and many other fine points. The psychiatrist will likely arrange for some basic laboratory tests of urine and blood samples, the number and type of which will depend upon his initial impressions of the nature of your problem or his subsequent findings.

In a few cases, the psychiatrist may require some very specialized examinations. These are made in the less common cases when there is a possibility that the problem may be due to organic (physical) changes in the body, (infections, tumor, hemorrhage, toxin, etc.) particularly those that are within or directly affect the nervous system. One of these is the making of a photographic tracing of minute differences in the so-called "brain waves" by a complicated machine with wires applied to various parts of the head in order to record variations in electrical action within the brain. The tracing, called an electro-encephalogram, shows up some types of abnormal activity in the brain. In rare cases, an air encephalograph is made: This is an x-ray picture of the brain (sometimes these are also made of the spinal cord) made after air has been injected into the space around the brain. In an ordinary x-ray picture of the head, the brain doesn't show up at all. However, the brain and spinal cord are normally surrounded by a fluid. When this fluid is drained off and an equal amount of air injected, the differences in the shadows on the x-ray, caused by the air, outlines the surface of and normal cavities of the brain (or spinal cord). Much more often than either an electroencephalogram or air encephalograph, the psychiatrist will want to examine the spinal fluid chemically. Obtaining it is a relatively simple procedure, carried out by introducing a hollow needle into the spinal canal between two vertebrae.

There's a special point about the psychiatrist's examination: It is the most extensive and by far the most time-consuming examination of any specialized field in medicine. The physician who specializes in skin disease can in many instances look at a rash and with the answers to three or four questions be quite certain of the nature of the disorder and its indicated treatment. Similarly, the physician specializing in nose and throat work can often examine the area of complaint, spot the trouble in a few moments and know what to do about it. But the psychiatrist if he is to help you effectively, must know a great deal about both your past and present life, your feelings, your methods of thinking, in addition to all the data about your physical and chemical status.

After having read this book, one should be able to understand better why the examination of the mental life of a person takes a comparatively long time. The psychiatrist must know as many facts as possible about the early development of the personality—those experiences in psychosexual development about which we have talked. He must be informed about your methods of defense— your flight and fight reactions. He will investigate in some detail your likes and dislikes, your loves and hates. Throughout his examination he will be noting your past and present use of the mental mechanisms and the methods you have developed to relate yourself to those about you, and what these relations are. All of these findings will help him understand your present "complaint" or difficulty.

Once the examination is completed, the psychiatrist. just like any other physician, will probably tell you what's wrong, and give you his recommendations as to what you ought to do about your problem or what he might be able to do about it. In some instances patients are brought to him who are too sick to be interested in coming on their own initiative or to help him reach a diagnosis. In such cases, he has to give his recommendations to the parents or other responsible relatives who can see that they are carried out.

TREATMENT

Psychiatric treatment covers a wide range of procedures. At best we can only touch superficially on some of these. *Psychotherapy* is the psychiatrist's chief method of treatment; since there are many different types of it, it is more correct to say that *they* are his chief methods.

Translated literally, Psychotherapy means "psychological treatment." A broad definition of Psychotherapy would include any type of device or relationship which the physician might use to improve the psychological aspect of his patient's illness. The term is used variously to include such relatively simple procedures as suggestion, or instruction, or sometimes just counsel and advice. It is used also to apply to very technical procedures such as *Psychoanalysis* and *Hypnosis*.

Some psychiatrists use the term Psychotherapy to cover all the relationships that occur between the doctor and the patient because, good or bad, those relationships are vital to any help that can be given.

If the patient goes to a hospital where he is engaged in various activities such as occupations, education, exercises, or recreation, the relationship of the patient to the hospital people who run those activities is also important and it too can be regarded in the broad sense as psychotherapy.

All patients with psychological problems should have some type or types of Psychotherapy. Sometimes it isn't effective. Sometimes it can be carried out only under very special conditions or by very special methods. The use of any complicated form requires extensive experience on the part of the therapist. The encouragement and instructions given a person with a sore throat are simple compared to the psychotherapy needed by the person who fears that the world is full of tuberculosis germs waiting to pounce on him.

The Psychotherapy for a small child is a quite different procedure from that for a mature adult. In fact those who practice it require a special training. Consequently, there are psychiatrists (and psychoanalysts) who work only with children.

Actually, Psychotherapy is used by every physician, from the country doctor to the specialized surgeon, sometimes intentionally, sometimes unknowingly. The simpler forms, or perhaps one should say the less technical forms, include all communications from the physician to his patient, which explain, reassure, suggest, give specific instructions or counsel.

Very often the most important feature of medication

may be the psychological understanding the patient has been given about it by his physician. Pink pills and colored water often have greater psychological than physiological significance.

There is also a very definite psychological effect in many forms of treatment of ills that involve rubbing, anointing and various kinds of manipulation of parts of the body. Because a lot of people want to think they can be "cured" by some form of handling there are thousands of fakers who operate various "rackets" to the distress of qualified men and often to the regret of their so-called patients.

Because there is so much misunderstanding about them, a discussion of specific types of technical psychotherapy should be of general interest. First, *Psychoanalysis*. This word has three meanings. It is a research procedure to investigate human thinking processes, emotions and behavior. It is a psychological theory of personality structure and function which we have discussed at length in this book. Finally, it is a treatment technique.

By means of this technique the patient can become aware of the unconscious elements in his emotional conflicts. Under the guidance of a psychoanalyst he can discover for himself their nature. In a series of daily sessions (over a period of months), the patient is encouraged to talk freely about any and everything that comes to his mind ("free association"). He forms a relationship with the analyst which becomes an important object of study during the course of the analysis because it represents the pattern of his relationships with other people. Under the analyst's guidance, the patient gains a clearer understanding of these. The psychoanalyst searches for evidence of unconscious wishes and strivings in their expression in words or actions, dreams and fantasies, relationships and interests, emotions related and displayed. He must be alert to hidden meanings, implications, lapses of memory, slips of the tongue, and all the subtle clues to the patient's real inner self. These the analyst has been trained to detect and understand. He watches for similar patterns of reaction in separate islands of experience. At appropriate times, he interprets his observations to the patient, and serves somewhat as a continuing signpost of directions for the patient's further excavations into his unconscious.

Before treatment the psychologically ill patient is like a fearful, struggling person in an unfamiliar and totally darkened room, crowded with furniture. He bumps into a chair and it falls over; he sidesteps and hits a lamp, which crashes. He struggles against unseen threatening enemies (the unconscious and therefore unknown forces in himself). With the gradual coming of light (the interpretations made by the analyst) the patient can see and evaluate those "threatening enemies" accurately. It then becomes his responsibility to put his house in order.

Unfortunately, the procedure as described above is extremely expensive in time and therefore money. It often takes many months and even years, even when the patient sees the analyst three to five times a week. Rarely is an *analysis* completed in less than 250 hours and often runs to 600 or 700 hours. Furthermore, it can be applied to only a small number of all the patients with psychiatric problems.

There are therefore *modifications* in practice. The principles of Psychoanalysis—an understanding of the unconscious, of personality dynamics, of the influence of the early childhood training and experiences, of repression and of the mental mechanisms—can be helpfully applied to even very short-term contacts *if* the psychiatrist is sufficiently familiar with psychoanalytic theory and practice. However, applying psychoanalytic principles to psychotherapy lasting an hour or a few hours is not Psychoanalysis.

Hypnosis is another type of psychotherapy which is more often used as a method of investigation. It is a form of suggestion, which the psychiatrists with special experience can use. By concentrating the patient's attention, with firm suggestion, the psychiatrist can place his patient in a trance-like state. When a person is under Hypnosis, it's possible to draw facts from him that he cannot remember or does not know in his normal conscious state. Furthermore, he will often accept suggestions from the therapist and carry them out later when he returns to his normal consciousness. But the effectiveness of Hypnosis as a psychotherapeutic method is relatively limited and may be dangerous unless employed by a skilled person.

Narcosynthesis or *psychotherapy under sedation*: When a patient is given an injection of a sedative slowly, he reaches a twilight state between wakefulness and deep sleep. Under encouragement he can recall and even relive experiences which he cannot remember in his normal conscious state. While semi-conscious, the emotional feeling related to these repressed memories can be expressed. Its meaning can be interpreted to the patient both at that time and again when he becomes fully conscious.

This method of treatment is particularly effective when the patient's distress is connected with a harrowing emotional experience in the recent past. For this reason it was a valuable therapeutic method for combat soldiers who became neuropsychiatric casualties. Its use in solving the emotional problems of ordinary civilian life is limited because the conflicts are frequently so well developed and firmly imbedded.

Psychiatric hospital treatment may be necessary for those patients who need a haven from the stresses and pressures of their ordinary life situation. Or when the patient's illness is such that he may prove dangerous to other's lives and property, then obviously hospitalization is necessary. Treatment (not merely custody) is needed and therefore every modern psychiatric hospital has facilities and staff essential for occupational and recreational activities, educational classes, music, art, gardening, etc. All of these are tools—therapeutic methods—for the patient to use in making his recovery.

Other treatment measures that the psychiatrist uses, almost always in the hospital, are various forms of what is known as *shock*. In connection with a certain mental illness it was discovered some twenty years ago that if a patient was given a sufficient amount of insulin (the secretion from the pancreas) hypodermically it lowered his blood sugar to a point where he became unconscious. This was called a shock. If the shock was intense enough, he might have a mild convulsion. After two, three, four or more hours, he could be given orange juice or some other form of sugar and be returned to his normal conscious state. It was further discovered that if, in certain types of illness, this procedure was carried out on each day for a period of four to eight weeks, the patient greatly improved.

On the assumption that the convulsion was the beneficial factor in the treatment, other methods for producing a convulsive attack were sought. Initially, certain drugs were used for this purpose. These were abandoned when it was discovered that a brief convulsive attack could be induced by a very momentary *electric shock* passed between the frontal lobes of the brain. Experience has shown that, in a limited variety of mental illnesses, it can be, and usually is, very effective. Ordinarily, such treatment may be given once every other day for a series of eight or ten or even more shocks. The physiologic or psychologic mechanisms of how this works are still not clear. Most psychiatrists believe that such treatments should be supplemented with psychological help, i.e. psychotherapy.

The psychiatrist makes use of many other specific

methods of treatment, many of which are limited to hospital use.

Sedation therapy. This treatment was used extensively in the army for acutely ill psychiatric battle casualties. It consists essentially of putting a person to sleep with various sedative drugs and keeping him asleep, sometimes for twenty-four hours, sometimes for as long as a month. He is permitted to wake up only enough to be fed two meals a day and to take care of physiological needs. Then he is put back to sleep again.

Various forms of *Physiotherapy*, that is treatment by physical measures (massage, ultraviolet light, the use of water in baths and showers—called *Hydrotherapy*) have long been used extensively for psychiatric patients, chiefly because of their sedative or tonic effects. One of the standard procedures in most psychiatric institutions is the use of what is known as the prolonged immersion tub in which a patient is kept in water of about body temperature from one to several hours at a time.

Heat or fever therapy is used regularly in the treatment of nervous system syphilis. Fever is induced sometimes by the use of malaria which gives the individual a chill and bout of fever every other day; sometimes the patient is placed in a specially constructed cabinet that is heated by electric lights; sometimes an electric blanket is used.

A brain operation known as the *prefrontal lobotomy* was devised in recent years for some very intractable forms of mental illness. Used judiciously, it has produced good results in some cases.

It is essential, however, that one understand that certain treatment is beneficial to certain types of illness. In heart disease certain medicines are indicated; in kidney disease other medications are indicated. The treatment applied for heart disease doesn't affect the kidney, or vice versa. Similarly each of the many different types of mental illness requires different treatment. Therefore all of the above-mentioned types of treatment have very specific and, as a consequence, limited applications, depending upon the kind, degree and duration of the illness.

There is another precaution that should be taken by any individual seeking psychiatric help. The problem of finding the right doctor is never an easy one at best. The job of finding a specialist in any field is even more difficult, that is, if you want to be sure you're getting into the hands of a competent and ethical person.

By all odds, the best method is to consult your own family physician and ask his advice. If he doesn't know one, he at least knows how he can find a psychiatrist who is competent. In the case that you don't know any physician, it is a legitimate question to ask the psychiatrist you expect to consult whether or not he belongs to the American Medical Association, and, more important, whether or not he belongs to the American Psychiatric Association. If he doesn't, be cautious! Non-membership doesn't totally disqualify him, but you will need good reasons why he is not and high recommendations about his ability from someone qualified to judge. Furthermore, it's perfectly legitimate to ask your psychiatrist if he is a diplomate of the American Board of Psychiatry and Neurology. This, too, isn't an absolute criterion of competence, but it is reasonably sure indication of his standing in the medical profession and his specialty.

If one is looking for a psychoanalyst, if he is really well qualified, he is almost sure to be a member of the American Psychoanalytic Association, which probably has the most rigid requirements for admission of any medical group in the United States. Many years ago, the Association accepted into its membership a very few non-medical ("lay") analysts. These were highly trained and competent persons, already accepted in the European analytic societies before coming to America. For several years, however, the American Psychoanalytic Association has accepted only physicians as members.

Perhaps even more difficult than finding the competent specialist for the average layman who has had no contact with the field whatever, is the task of locating a psychiatric hospital which provides treatment. It's an unfortunate fact that because of public apathy, the great majority of our state psychiatric hospitals are totally inadequate in staff, greatly overcrowded, exist on a disgracefully small budget of cost per patient and do little more than provide custody. Unfortunately, a considerable number of private institutions capitalize on the fact that many individuals hesitate or are fearful of taking their relatives or friends to a state institution. There *are* many very good private hospitals but there are too many others which provide little more than custody on a more elaborate scale. Therefore, get the best information you can about the qualifications and reputation of the persons running the institution in which you are interested.

This problem of seeking professional help brings up a specific question. If one has a psychological difficulty, why should he not consult a psychologist? After all, the psychologist knows a good deal about the psychology of people. Therefore, one might assume that he is an expert in dealing with psychological difficulties.

Psychology and *Psychiatry* are two words that are often confused. They sound somewhat alike and their special fields of interest are closely related. Psychologists have specialized particularly in the determination of abilities and modes of reaction as they can be measured by objective tests. Such tests have been created for the purpose of measuring intelligence, special abilities, etc., etc. Through their observations and experiments, psychologists have been able to formulate laws of learning, habit formation, and many other psychological processes. They have described thought processes.

Many psychological problems, however, involve mental health, as well as an understanding of mental phenomena. One cannot evaluate the total person by considering the psychological life separately from the physical condition and the body chemistry. Knowledge of the interrelationship of all of the aspects of the personality are essential for an understanding interpretation of behavior. Therefore, in all cases where health and ill health are concerned, the physician (including the psychiatrist) should assume full responsibility.

It is not always so easy to see difficult choices and decisions and activities that may vitally affect happiness as health problems. Pre-marriage, or for that matter post-marriage counselling may or may not directly involve health. Vocational choice, school adjustment, parental education, job placement—these and other matters very often do not have an obvious medical aspect. Again, they may. When they do not, many individuals without medical or psychiatric training who are competently trained and experienced, can give valuable advice. When the person giving such help has ready access to psychiatric advice, all concerned benefit.

A sub-specialist in the field of psychology is a clinical (i.e. having to do with patients) psychologist who works very closely with the psychiatrist in the diagnosis and treatment of psychiatric patients. The results of a certain group of tests he uses show a cross-section view of the personality at the time of testing. These were mentioned as part of the psychiatric examination, and are extremely valuable in arriving at the diagnosis of psychological illness. The clinical psychologist is invaluable and bears somewhat the same relation to the psychiatrist as does the roentgenologist (x-ray physician) to the surgeon; his test findings provide diagnostic help and corroborative evidence to support or add to the psychiatrist's clinical findings.

Some clinical psychologists who are technically trained can give psychological treatment for mental illnesses. But the accepted standard of practice of such individuals, as outlined by their own leaders, is to have a close association with a physician or a group of physicians.

An instruction: Keep in mind, that there are probably more quacks and charlatans presuming to help persons with emotional illnesses than in any other field of health. Beware! If your problem is one that affects your mental or physical health, seek medical opinion. If it is one which advice alone can help solve, there are many experts whom you may consult, including your pastor.

A Warning: Be extremely cautious (and leery) about seeking advice of anyone who *advertises* himself merely as a "psychotherapist" or "psychoanalyst," whether it be in a phone book listing, the newspaper, or the sign on the "office door."

Before we leave the subject of treatment, perhaps no misconception in psychiatry is more widespread than the fact that most individuals who have had a mental illness cannot get well, or that those who do remain something of a liability to themselves or their families or their communities. The great, great majority of psychiatric patients recover! A high percentage of the psychiatric battle casualties returned to combat duty! In fact, there is probably no other group of illnesses in any specialty which has a higher record of recovery than the psychiatric ones. This recovery rate is undoubtedly improving as psychiatric experience and knowledge increases. Also it will increase as people become more intelligent about psychiatry and seek help sooner rather than wait for the machinery to be completely broken down.

CHAPTER IX

THE APPLICATION TO YOU

HAVING STAYED with this book this far, and having followed our attempt to explain as simply as we can how you and I click or fail to click, you might ask logically, "What is in it for me?" It does us little good to know what it is that makes one man's stomach ache and leads another man to write a sonnet. We want to know how that knowledge applies to us.

Whether you can apply the knowledge depends upon many things. It depends first on how well we may have confused you or clarified things for you about how you function. It depends on how honest you can be about yourself. It depends a little on your I.Q.

As a parting shot we want to try to summarize under three headings some suggestions about ways to maintain mental health:

First, accept the reality that life is a struggle. It requires continuous adjustment both within ourselves, and between ourselves and the rest of the world.

Second, if we are going to survive that struggle we have to find security in our environment. That means we have to learn how to balance the emotional stresses against the emotional supports.

Third, we have to find satisfaction, fun and happiness if we are going to stay healthy.

THE STRUGGLE

By struggle we mean just that; life is a two-part struggle. A fight goes on constantly within ourselves about whom we love, whom we hate, whether we will do what we want to do or what we should do, whether we should be selfish or unselfish, whether we should be juvenile or adult.

Another fight goes on between ourselves and the external world, as we try to meet its demands, try to do what is expected of us, try to do what we know we want to do, sometimes against great odds.

Constantly present in this struggle there are two important factors, that all too often we tend to forget. In the first place none of us exist in a vacuum. We have to be social beings and that means that everything we do has a relation to other people. Our behavior reflects on them and theirs on us. Whether by way of neurotic symptoms or "normal" responses, we always interact. Mental health as well as emotional upsets and mental illness have a very direct relationship to the people around us.

In the second place we can't *really* see ourselves either as we actually are or as other people see us. Consequently, what we think and feel about ourselves or about others is modified by many things about which we can have no knowledge. Therefore, in understanding this struggle we must see that what we or other people say and do isn't necessarily what it appears to be on the surface.

In spite of the limitations of self-evaluation, it is wise to attempt to size-up ourselves—to take inventory or stock now and then. We can't be sure just what some of our behavior means but, at least if we are willing to do so, we can face up to our reactions honestly. For instance we can:

Admit our own weaknesses to ourselves and con-
sider how to strengthen or balance them.
Avoid fooling ourselves about our prejudices and
hypocrisy.
Look for our ambivalences.
Analyze our hates and look for constructive outlets
for them.
Accept responsibility for our own failures.
See if we are using our talents to the best advantage.

In doing this we do not need to be overly introspective;
nor should we run ourselves down in the hope (perhaps
unconscious) that we can invite reassurance or a denial
of our failure from our friends; nor should we deny our
faults and misbehavior. The sickest mental patient is the
one who most hotly denies that there is anything wrong
with him.

A person has to *learn* to be objective about himself.
Self-evaluation may be entirely useless if it is biased by
insecurity or conceit or insincerity or frank dishonesty.
Then it is not only a waste of time but it may be very
harmful.

Despite our weaknesses and our neurotic mechanisms
the great majority of us get along in the world reasonably
well. Most of us, most of the time, live in relative peace
with ourselves and stay within the accepted range of behavior of our social group. Even though we all react
"badly" at times, we are included in the class generally
referred to as "normal."

Certain behavior signals maladjustment whether in
ourselves or in others. It is a "red light," warning evidence
of temporary personality failure or perhaps of serious mental illness, depending upon its intensity and persistence.
It may be unwise to make a list of such danger signals,
for some people are very suggestible, like the *Three*

Men in a Boat by Jerome K. Jerome. While adrift without oars, they read the medical dictionary, which happened to be in the boat, to pass the time. They concluded that between them they had every disease except "old maid's house knee."

However, if we can see these signs of difficulty in adjustment for what they are, we can often do something ourselves or call upon family or friends to help us solve the problem facing us before it can make us seriously ill. We may need to call for professional assistance when the "symptoms" recur frequently, last for days or weeks, cause intense emotional distress which we cannot relieve on our own. When severe they are truly indications of serious trouble, which the sooner investigated, the easier relieved.

Just as good physical health is indicated by the absence of symptoms, so is good mental health. If the answers to the following questions are all "No," we can assume that we are mentally healthy.

Are you always worrying?

Are you unable to concentrate because of unrecognized reasons?

Are you continually unhappy without justified cause?

Do you lose your temper easily and often?

Are you troubled by regular insomnia?

Do you have wide fluctuations in your moods, from depression to elation, back to depression, which incapacitates you?

Do you continually dislike to be with people?

Are you upset if the routine of your life is disturbed?

Do the children consistently get "on your nerves?"

Are you "browned off," and constantly bitter?

Are you afraid without real cause?

Are you always right and the other person always wrong?

Do you have numerous aches or pains for which no
doctor can find a physical cause?

If you answer any of these questions in the positive
then something *is* wrong with you. Our sober advice is
to seek help.

There is one other question we might ask ourselves.
To it we would all answer "yes." Do we feel depressed
when we are excluded or rejected? Does that make us
feel sometimes that we're a failure in contrast with others
around us? An affirmative answer would be that of an
average person. All of us are rejected or slighted or denied
more or less often. When that happens we are inclined
to compare ourselves unfavorably with the people who
appear to be "in." We develop what are sometimes called
inferiority feelings. These are an expression of insecurity
that we will discuss a little later.

As children, when the folks didn't seem to appreciate
us, at one time or another many of us threatened to run
away from home in order to make them feel sorry for
what they had done to us. As adults we may want to
withdraw from social contact when not accepted by those
whose approval we want. Or, do the opposite—fight back.
Disappointments in love, not receiving an invitation to a
party or to join a fraternity or club or lodge may hurt
some of us terribly. All of us want to belong,—as proof
that we are loved and enjoyed and appreciated. When
we are not included our thoughts become clogged with
questions and answers: "What is wrong with me?" "They
are unfair." "Didn't I wear the right dress?" Etc., etc., etc.

It is easy to mull over and stew about such rejections,
blaming our own inadequacy, accusing others, and generally feeling sorry for ourselves. We may even become
convinced that we aren't what we ought to be and worry
about how to change. Some of the more objective-minded
of us may see the problem as one of orientation to a blow

to our pride. Our belief in ourselves suffers when others do not appreciate us. There is a tendency to turn our thoughts too much toward self-denunciation which so often leads us into a depression. Sometimes we turn upon those who reject us and by forcing ourselves upon them bid for another rejection.

Probably the most constructive thing to do, often only possible through strong determination, is to seek other people, individually or in groups, or activities or job from which we can gain satisfaction. We can always fall back on true and tried sources of affection or interest. We can also help ourselves with rationalizing in the way the fox did about the grapes in Aesop's fable: those who rejected us weren't what we thought they were anyway, and there is the chance that this may be true. Finally, we can develop a philosophy, and a very sensible one it is, that potential pals or sweethearts and exclusive groups are a little like street cars—another one comes along every seven minutes if we watch for it.

Only when the sense of rejection or inferiority is chronic or recurs with too little and too frequent provocation is one apt to need professional advice. Our emotions get so deeply involved that usually we don't act upon, or even listen to our own cold-blooded best judgment. In the normal course of events, when we become overly introspective about our difficulties, it is well to keep in front of us the fact that intellectual understanding can help us if we will admit it and take action. There's a saying that the voice of the intelligence is weak but that it is persistent. By its persistence it can, in varying degrees, overcome emotional pressure. Unhealthy reactions always have a definite relationship to developmental experiences of insecurity, dependency, previous rejections. With a clearer understanding of the personality, the reader can re-enforce his intelligence in arriving at the solutions of such emotional problems. For overcoming an emotional block one must strengthen the positive aspects which are present even in the darkest situations.

We don't outlive our struggles. No matter what may have happened or what will happen, they will continue. However, many of the sharpest thorns, the most difficult problems, had their origin back in childhood. The moral is, that one of our chief obligations, insofar as we can learn how, is to make the struggle that our children may have less difficult for them. We can't reiterate here the many specific suggestions that we gave with regard to the psychosexual stages of development or the object choices (persons) at various stages of life. However, there are some generalities which could bear re-emphasis.

Our children are going to be what we make them. Their relationship with others is going to be happy and successful only if we have loved them and encouraged their development towards emotional as well as physical maturity. This implies that we haven't smothered them with nor have we starved them for our attentions. We give them our selfishness or our bigotry, our broad vision and understanding or our prejudices.

Since childhood patterns stay with us through a lifetime, it is almost impossible to over-emphasize the importance of treating a child like a human being. The golden rule is an excellent standard for parent-child relationships. We haven't any right to force our demands on him just because he is the smaller. We can hardly be rude to our children and not expect them to be rude to us. The same is true when we are considerate or inconsiderate, thoughtful or thoughtless, respectful or disrespectful, loving or indifferent.

Treating a child like a human being doesn't mean that the parents give up the use of and indoctrination of discipline. But one has to have a much broader concept of discipline than to regard it solely as a means of coercion through edicts and whippings. Nor should one think of discipline only in terms of negative features—denials, refusals, punishment. It is a tool that the parents need to use, a tool that the child will have to learn to use in the management of his own life. A disciplined personality is one with self-control. A parent must base his enforcement of externally applied discipline on his conviction of the importance of the solution he proposes for the problem at hand. He should present an explanation of it and its importance which is adequate to the child's age and the circumstances. The child's point of view should always receive parental consideration. So used, parental discipline can serve as an aid in the child's acceptance of personal and social responsibility.

The parent has the big job of helping the child handle his ambivalences—the conflicts which he tries to resolve by answering yes and no at the same time. These start early, they arise sometimes because of fear, sometimes from lack of knowledge, very often from lack of experience.

Another parental responsibility is the obligation to stimulate the child's motivation, at least the conscious part of it, for whatever job has to be done. Most often the child's motivation is related to the way the parent himself may feel about the subject at hand. We all need short-time and long-time goals and it is the parent's opportunity to help the child pick these and work towards them and overcome the obstacles in the way which are too great for his childish abilities. Sometimes this means discussing the matter with him, sometimes it means playing with him, sometimes it means working wth him. It always means loving him.

Still another task for parents is to help the child to recognize and admit reality. This may mean beginning with the admission of it to themselves, even to revising their opinions about their own children. The average healthy parent tends to overevaluate his children, to hurry them too fast, to expect too much of them, to assume that they are much above the "average," to set standards by what the neighbors will think rather than by what is best for the child and the family.

Ideally, the home is a protected and friendly environment in which the parent can prepare his child to recognize reality and meet the world without disillusionment or the handicap of ignorance and inexperience.

SECURITY

Security is one of the pillars upon which mental health rests. We can't be pat in stating ways of how to find it. Security isn't just a matter of money because millionaires can feel extremely insecure. Nor is it merely a matter of having a bed and some food because many people with those lead miserably insecure lives.

There are really two basic securities that a man seeks —and needs. The first of these is the inner harmony of the personality, the resolution of tension between different parts of himself. No matter what the external environment is if he isn't at peace within himself, he doesn't have security.

A second basic need has to do with love. A man who is loved is really secure. He who is fortunate enough to be loved has, in most cases, earned it; he has been mature enough to give it and, therefore, he has received interest on the investment of his emotion by receiving love from others.

Unfortunately, the world has too many people in it who want to love others and to make friends, but who don't know how. Because of their childhood experience they are afraid to break out of the little cages they have built around themselves both consciously and unconsciously. Those who can't love at all are hopelessly sick. It is a sign of real maturity when an individual gains greater satisfaction out of loving than out of being loved. He who really loves—gives of himself—never has to worry about being loved.

Security depends upon the extent and type of demands of the environment in addition to one's internal peace of mind. It is contingent upon how we handle these and whether we can marshal enough resources to satisfy them. Sometimes it is a little difficult for people to know how to obtain security for the personality. To explain, let us consider an analogy, economic security. We know very well that economic security doesn't just happen. We must make plans for it, we must pay attention to the reality situation and spend according to the limits of our resources, what we need, and what we can (and do) get. Therefore, we need to know the extent of our resources and our capabilities. Ordinarily, we set up a goal, and then work towards its achievement. We decide upon our own purposes for achieving that goal—what we are saving our money for, how we are going to use it, how we can use it to the best advantage. We have to plan carefully. Once we have a reserve, it gives us a sense of power and freedom and elasticity. It is something to draw on in emergencies. We have to follow the same general principles to obtain any type of security we feel we need, whether it is personal or family or social or physical or economic. Set a goal. Make a plan for attaining it. Develop reserves. Keep working at the program.

Let us apply these principles specifically to the conscious part of the personality. First we have to see what we have: our assets, our needs, in what areas we feel secure and where insecure. Depending upon what we find, we have to make plans as to how we are going to satisfy our unmet needs for security. Then we can look at what we want and set a goal which may have reference to the number of friends we wish, the hope for a family, business expansion, the size of the bank account, or satisfactions from a hobby. Once we have determined our goal we have a motive, a purpose, a sense of direction, for our efforts. We must also weigh carefully the influence in the environment which will force a modification in our original desires. In order to achieve our aim we may have to learn some new techniques and may have to explore new fields of interest, compromise with the environment, and learn our way by trial and error.

Because the human personality does have so many facets, the sense of security in one may carry over and support a minor insecurity in another one. It is a little like having diversified economic investments. If one of them goes bad, it doesn't ruin the investor. If insecurity develops in relation to a job, we will hope that security at home may give sufficient support to provide the confidence, encouragement and reassurance necessary to carry on till the job straightens out.

Parents have a special responsibility for providing the security that children need, both internal and external. If we feel secure ourselves, we instill it in them. If we do not feel secure, we can't help but make our children feel insecure. Psychiatrists agree that in the case of mal adjusted small children, very often the parent needs treatment as much or more than the child. Sometimes the child of secure parents may find false reasons for inse curity. This, parental understanding can usually correct

SATISFACTION

Another one of the pillars of mental health is a recognition of the need that we all want and must have *Satisfaction*. We have explained that the struggle of life isn't always what it appears on the surface because of our unconscious motives. If we can direct these reasonably successfully to acceptable and practical social goals, we will be able to find security. In the last analysis security rests heavily on finding satisfaction. The two are inseparably intertwined.

As we have seen, our minds play tricks on us. We have tried to illustrate them. Some of them result in healthy satisfactions; some in distorted satisfactions. Whether we find healthy satisfaction depends on many factors, not the least of which is the ability to produce it for ourselves. But here again one may be handicapped because he never learned sufficient independence; he grew up dependent on others to find and provide security and satisfactions. Or he may be handicapped by an immature, aggressive, demanding nature. So suggestions as to how to find satisfaction may be useless for such persons. Besides, there are no simple rules about how to find it. There are helpful, wise old sayings that too often we don't apply to ourselves. "You get out about what you put in." "Your return is directly proportionate to the wisdom and size of your investment." "No field will grow corn without the help of God, some seed and a lot of hard work."

We can make bad investments of our love, effort or interest which bring us unhappiness instead of satisfaction. Everybody does so sometimes. If we make them frequently, however, there is something wrong with us. The chances are that no simple advice is going to bring about a change in our practices until we find out through professional help what the cause of our difficulty may be. But for those persons who can use them, we can suggest some advice about investments that do pay good returns. Those who feel the need for more satisfaction than they now have might consider them.

Exact some fun from whatever we have to do. For most people, much of their lives are filled with relatively uninteresting chores. There is no use denying this. For instance, the modern household routine in itself is not satisfying to housewives. Nevertheless, many a home-maker finds satisfaction in being the one who administers a home that is free of friction and disorder and thus she adds to the enjoyment of the family when they are in the home.

If we are chronically dissatisfied in a job, perhaps it is the wrong job for us. However, we should be sure that there isn't something wrong with our ability to accept the cards that are dealt before we call for a new deal. Maybe our lack of satisfaction is due to a feeling that we are not properly appreciated. In that case we must be honest enough to consider whether it is the way we may have done the job that has been the cause of the failure to evoke praise or approval. A good principle is that giving satisfaction, whether it is to our family, or our employer, or our friends, begets it.

If required activity fails to provide satisfaction, get it from a source of our own choosing. This is really a further elaboration of the point made above. We can't escape some drudgery, some monotony, some unpleasant things that we have to do but we do not have to depend entirely on one source for satisfaction. Because we have *some* things that we *have* to do, doesn't mean that we can't find a good many things that we would like and want to do. Again, like the diversification of investments, the satisfaction from the chosen source can often compensate for its lack in the "must" jobs.

Vary the diet. We can't live on a diet of fish and carrots nor a program of all work and no play. We need new activities, new contacts, new scenes, new experiences, new friends. All of these are potential sources of additional satisfaction. If we want to feel sorry for ourselves, we can stay in our own little foxholes and let the rest of the world go by, enjoying our lonesomeness and our misery. It may take special planning to read a book or tat some lace or practice a tennis serve or drive to California but the chances are that any of these will pay well in satisfaction for that extra effort.

Learn to play. There are few stupidities greater than

that of the man or woman who prides himself or herself on never playing. His unbroken devotion to work, his unbalanced compulsions to keep his nose to the grindstone with never a letup for restful relaxation in sports, hobbies or avocations, is foolish. Once in a long while this attitude is due to ignorance, occasionally to necessity.

There are men and women among us who promise themselves that they will grind away until they are "in a position" to relax and enjoy themselves, but they never seem to reach that point. It is really far better for us to pause now and then, in order to enjoy a little fun and relaxation along the way. This can make life more pleasant for us and those we love than to reject current recreation for some imagined future, permanent vacation. Men and women who won't take time out of their lives to play occasionally are usually the ones who neglect their wives, husbands or children with the same self-deception that they will make it all up to them in a lump some day. Most of them never get around to doing so.

In addition to these instructions for the adult, we have a word or two of advice to parents. We must keep in mind that the little baby starts out as a lone wolf. Most of his initial satisfactions are primitive and so he has to learn a game of substitution by the time he is two or three years of age. It is our job to help him find socially approved substitutions which satisfy him. One of his big lessons that is so important in becoming an adult is that as a child, he has to learn that he can't always have what he wants when he wants it. He also must learn that future satisfaction may entail some delay in its realization, maybe even some discomfort or sacrifice at the moment. That is a most difficult and basic lesson; even many of us as adults have not yet learned it well. Just as a child, we go on spending money or energy, as fast as we get it. Instead of making plans, we live only for the minute regardless of the consequences.

The most specific instruction about helping a child find satisfaction is to work or play with him until he can find it on his own. In the meantime he gets it from us or from what we do with him. In sharing ourselves with him we teach him how to share himself with others. We are wise if we involve the child in the enjoyment of our own avocation. On the other hand, the parent is missing a great opportunity when he looks upon his child's excursion into stamps or photography as some transient, unimportant "kid" interest instead of making it a vehicle of joint interest. Versatility and range of activities are pretty largely determined in childhood experience and in turn are dependent upon the parental interest, guidance and support. It stands oldsters in good stead to have a life-long habit of being interested in new ideas and activities.

FINALE

This book has been almost entirely about you and me. In a sense it has been a narcissistic one because it has concerned just ourselves, and our interest in ourselves. We hope it has been helpful in providing information that may prove personally useful.

Behind this discussion of and about ourselves and much, much broader than it, is the hope that somehow by understanding ourselves better we can improve our interpersonal relationships. We hope that from a better individual understanding we can derive a stronger social consciousness and greater ability to live at peace with other people.

As we indicated in the introduction, when we look around us we see on all sides homes broken by divorce or separation, increasing juvenile delinquency, crime waves, expressions of group hatreds, political wranglings, international distrust and "cold" wars. One result of the war was a keener awareness of and interest in the nature of the man's personality. But most of the war's influence followed the trend of the last twenty-five years in giving a far greater impetus to the development of our technical knowledge of gadgets and machines.

We believe that our highest priority of study and research in our present world should be given to the "know why" and the "know how" of getting along with ourselves and others.

Our American "know how" of technical developments carried us through a great and difficult war successfully. It cost a tremendous investment (and waste) of money and manpower. Surely it is possible that if the individual American could have and apply the "know why" and "know how" of himself and his understanding of people, he would help carry us through what looms as a difficult peace. We must either learn how to get along with people or else just accept the inevitability of another world plan for killing and being killed.

Democracy is founded on a belief in the power and dignity of the individual. If our way of life is to survive, it will be because we as individuals have made a study of ourselves. That means that after a good look at ourselves we will do something to get the kinks out of relationships that have become fouled up by our hatreds, jealousies, envies, selfishness, isolationism and immaturity.

The preamble of the charter of the cultural organization of the United Nations has in it this statement: ". . . wars begin in the minds of men . . ."

This means your mind and my mind. Maybe most important it means our children's minds because they introject all that they are directly from us. The only way to peace is by becoming more mature and raising a generation that is even more mature than we are. If we do not succeed, we are lost.